Maria C*

10 SECRETS TO SPEAKING ENGLISH

Dear Maria,

Your English is excellent! Thank you for being my friend, Best wishes to you and your family,

Dale Christinsen

Other Books by Dale Christensen

Patriot's Path (2014)
– a plan for our future

Dark Horse Candidate (2014)
– autobiography

A Disciple's Journey (2014)
– spiritual perspective and religious background

Guide to Greatness (2014)
– inspiration to bring out the greatness in everyone

Thoughts in Verse (2014)
– uplifting poetry

Out of Print:

The Shopping Center Acquisition Handbook (1984)
– complete process and documentation

Turning the Hearts Vol. I-IV *(1982)*
– family history from earliest ancestors to marriage

History of the Church in Peru (1991)
– selective personal and general highlights

Entrepreneur Guide: The Ultimate Business & Learning Experience (2001)
– textbook for MBA course

Teaching Improvement Program
– *USTC MBA Program & Business School* (2001)
– training for MBA professors

10 SECRETS TO SPEAKING ENGLISH

BY

Dale Christensen

10 Secrets to Speaking English

Published by:
Dale Christensen
Books@Dale2016.com

Cover design: Matt Christensen and Rachael Gibson
Editing Assistance: Jan Jackson and Susan Allen Myers

All rights reserved. No part of this book may be reproduced or transmitted in any form or by any means whatsoever without written permission from the author, except in the case of brief quotations embodied in critical articles and reviews.

Copyright © 2014 by Dale Christensen

Library of Congress, Catalog-in-Publication Data

ISBN:1517192560
Hardback: 978-xxxxxxxxxx
Softback: 978-1517192563
eBook: 978-xxxxxxxxxx
Audio: 978-xxxxxxxxxx

Printed in the United States of America
Year of first printing: 2014

Dedication

To all the Chinese people who want to speak English
and to those who teach them.
Dream your dreams
and stretch yourselves to new heights.
You can do it!

This book is dedicated to you,
to your dreams and to your efforts
in making those dreams become reality!

Acknowledgements

Thanks to all who have contributed and helped in preparing this book. Appreciation goes to all those who shared their ideas, experience and inspiration. Many thanks to those who helped prepare this transcript, to translate it from English into Chinese and in preparing the manuscript for publication. I acknowledge and congratulate all those who learned and are learning to speak English by using these simple secrets.

Table of Contents

Preface	1
STUDENT MANUAL	5
Student Manual - English	7
Student Manual - Chinese	19
Student Manual - Spanish	30
TEACHER'S MANUAL (English Only)	43
Prelude To Fluency	45
Chapter 1 – Confidence – Self Talk	69
Chapter 2 - Teach Others	78
Chapter 3 - Sing Songs	96
Chapter 4 - Talk to the TV & Radio	105
Chapter 5 - Read Aloud & Read A Lot	111
Chapter 6 - Call Others on the Telephone	126
Chapter 7 - Group Participation	133
Chapter 8 - Interpret For Others	141
Chapter 9 - Memorize New Vocabulary	146
Chapter 10 - Read, Write, and Memorize Poetry	161
Summary	178
About the Author	185

Preface

"When you measure your progress, your progress accelerates."
- Thomas S. Monson

I am not an English teacher! I don't want to teach English, but I can teach you how to speak English and how to speak it very well. You cannot learn to speak a language by learning the 'science of the language.'

You did not learn to speak Chinese that way. To learn to speak English you must just speak! Studying will help a little. Listening and reading will help some. But, learning grammar and all the rules of speaking correctly won't help you. In fact, at times, it will even impede your speaking fluency.

If you want to speak English, you must practice speaking. Just do it! Just speak, everyday!"

There is an optimistic anticipation that readers will include in their personal and business plans a dimension of humanitarian service. You readers can commit yourselves to having an abundance mentality and being an honorable participant and competitor while lifting and building others as you pursue their business goals and objectives. You will find great success and satisfaction.

If China is going to emerge as the world's leading nation, it needs to develop and be a leader in many ways. China and Chinese people will need to understand and implement the best business practices, education and communication. They will need to be the innovators and leaders in ideas, technology, service and language. China is beginning to experience, and is on the verge of, a great economic expansion and development phase never before experienced.

If China continues to be politically wise and patient and allows the spirit of entrepreneurship to grow in the hearts of the people, then the question is not "if" but "when" will China emerge as the number one leading economy and nation of the world. To do so, modern China will need to regain the spirit of ingenuity, innovation and creativity that was the hallmark of ancient China.

In doing business together, China and the United States and other nations, are like dance partners learning the steps and movements to old and new economic rhythms. It's an exciting adventure and a most enjoyable experience. We may occasionally step on each other's toes or move closer or farther apart in anticipation of each other's steps. But we can learn to move more gracefully, energetically and enjoyably to the economic waltzes, rock and roll or ballets of the marketplace. Communication and language are vital parts of this music.

Many years ago, while working as a waiter during my college years at Anthony's Pier 4 Restaurant in Boston, I overheard a group of businessmen talking very seriously over lunch. One man leaned forward in a very matter-of-fact way and said, "Look, no matter how you cut it, an apple is an apple. And that's the truth!" His words impressed me very much. That very day I wrote the following poem titled, "Truth Is Like An Apple":

An apple is an apple, no matter what the way
  You choose to eat or cut it, or the price you have to pay.
It may be green and bitter, or very sweet and red.
  It may be large and shiny or withered, small and dead.

You can carve that apple nicely or just leave it there to rot.
You can bake it in the oven, or stew it in a pot.
You can share it with a neighbor and make a real friend.
It's what you do with it that matters in the end.
Now truth is like that apple, it's very plain to see
If it's in your hand at present or in a distant tree.
So hold to the fruit of wisdom, and seek the simple truth;
For wherever it may be found, the truth is still the truth.

One truth we all can enjoy is that language helps us convey meaning. Speaking a common language can bring us closer together. The poet Edgar A. Guest eloquently wrote this in a poem he titled "Wisdom".

This is wisdom, maids and men,
knowing what to say and when.
Speech is common; thought is rare,
wise men choose their words with care.
Artists with the master touch,
never use one phrase too much.
Jesus, preaching on the Mount,
made His every sentence count.
Lincoln's Gettysburg address
needs not one word more or less.
This is wisdom, maids and men,
knowing what to say and when.

Speech is common; thought is rare, wise men choose their words with care.

We can learn how to speak and choose our words with care. In order to speak English, one must speak it every day. This takes effort and commitment.

Student's Manual

3 Languages

10 Secrets to Speaking English

Background

Chinese people study English for many years. They learn grammar and have a very good vocabulary, but they continue to have difficulty in speaking. There are several key obstacles that cause this phenomenon, and they can be quickly and easily overcome. One of the biggest obstacles is fear! Another obstacle is the need and habit to mentally translate from Chinese to English and then to convert these thoughts into spoken words and sentences. Much of the difficulty is caused by the way Chinese people study and learn the English Language.

Learning Language

<u>Learn to speak as a child learns to speak</u>. Learning to understand and speak a language is one of the first skills a child develops. Small children are capable of learning many languages at the same time. They listen for a time and then they try to repeat. Usually, their learning environment is very friendly and encouraging. Parents give great praise for the smallest efforts and slightest improvements. Therefore, the child develops courage and is excited about learning. Remember, it is a long time before they know anything about grammar, spelling or formal sentence structure. Their whole focus is on speaking and communicating.

<u>Language teachers should avoid criticism and be very encouraging and generous with praise</u>. If someone is lazy or doesn't like to learn to speak a new language, the best way to

motivate them is to praise them for their efforts and never criticize. Criticism or pointing out faults too often causes the student to be apprehensive and they lose self-confidence and develop fear of speaking.

<u>Learning to speak any language is a right brain activity</u>. Other right brain activities or qualities include physical movement and coordination, art, music, creativity and imagination. The left side of our brain masters the very orderly and structured things like memorization, mathematics, science, logical thinking, accounting etc. Young Chinese children learn to speak Chinese using the right side of their brain. But perhaps because the Chinese language requires a lot of memorization of Chinese characters etc. the science of the language is learned or understood in a very left brained manner.

<u>The Chinese educational system promotes left brain development</u>. Because of the very nature of the Chinese educational system's focus on learning information, memorizing, scientific focus and its testing and advancement methods, we find that Chinese students excel in these areas. However, these same students have great difficulty in being able to speak or otherwise verbalize the English language. Their greatest desire is to speak English fluently, but this is also their biggest fear. Most often, it is an obstacle or challenge too big for many to overcome. They continue to diligently study the science of the language and develop a large vocabulary and understanding of grammar rules, etc.

The "Mute" Language

The most diligent students of the English language are often frustrated because they just can't seem to access their knowledge and get it out of their mouth. For this reason, many of them call it a "mute" language. They understand it and can read and write it, but they cannot speak it!

Purpose

The purpose of the *Ten Secrets of Accelerated English Fluency* is to provide key principles, activities and methods of measurement that everyone can use to improve speaking ability. The goal of these secrets is to help people enjoy learning and fluently communicating in English. Speakers can now have tools and skills, along with a friendly environment where they can overcome their fears, enjoy and measure their progress through personal effort and/or competition with others.

Guarantee

If these methods are utilized correctly and followed diligently, participants are guaranteed that their speaking fluency will not only increase dramatically, but it will accelerate. You do not need a foreigner or native English speaker to improve your spoken English. Yes, that would be a wonderful advantage, but you can dramatically improve on your own by following these guidelines. That's a promise and a guarantee!

Scoring

Using charts to score your efforts will remind you to do the activity, require you to keep a record of your progress and will show you where you are putting the most effort and where you need to improve. At the end of each day or week simply give an honest and objective evaluation of how you did during that day or week. Give yourself a number score from 0 to 5 or from 0 to 10 in each activity area. The numbers can represent the following rating: 0 = no effort or failure to perform; 1 = very poor effort; 2 = little effort; 3 = not so good effort; 4 = below average; 5 = average; 6 = above average effort; 7 = very good effort; 8 = a lot of effort; 9 = excellent effort; 10 = perfect or maximum score available.

10 Secrets

1. <u>Confidence</u>: The most important aspect of speaking is having good confidence (faith in yourself and in God). Self-esteem is how you feel about yourself. It includes how you think and what you say to yourself or "self-talk". What you feel determines what you think and what you think determines what you say and how you say it. If you feel good about yourself, you will say good things and speak well. If you feel bad things about yourself, you will think negative thoughts. You will not have self-confidence. Instead you will have fear and you will not speak. When most Chinese people are asked how their English is or if they are told heir English is very good, they immediately respond by saying, "Oh, my English is very poor. I have no chance to practice." Do not say this to yourself and do not say it to others. If you say it often enough, you will begin to believe it and soon you will be paralyzed and unable to speak. You will begin to forget what you know because your right brain cannot speak or use the knowledge you have stored in your left brain. In learning to speak English, you must put the Chinese custom of modesty or humility aside. When someone compliments you, just say thank you. If someone asks how your English is or criticizes you, respond in a positive manner by saying something like, "I love to speak English". Or "My English is improving". Or "I am working very hard to improve my English". These positive statements will reinforce positive thoughts and good feelings. With increased confidence, you will overcome fear and speak more freely. Your mind is the most fantastic computer in the universe. Don't unplug it or give it deadly viruses by saying or thinking negative things to yourself or to others.

2. <u>Teach Others</u>: It is a known fact that the teacher learns more than the student. People receive more when they give.

When a person only receives they become crippled and soon die. When you teach someone else to speak English you forget yourself and concentrate on helping someone else. This is a key process in learning. You actually get more when you give more. You get better at speaking when you give others instructions and encouragement. Secondly, when you teach you are forced to utilize all the skills of speaking well. You must remember what you have stored in your left brain, transfer it to the right side, translate it from Chinese into English and then you are forced to verbalize it. You must speak it to teach it. You hear yourself speak and can recognize your own needs and correct yourself while you teach, correct and encourage your student(s). It's a great method and a self-motivating process.

For thousands of years, this method has been a powerful secret to learning. To compare the difference in just receiving or taking in the learning process, we can use the story told about two famous seas, the Sea of Galilee and the Dead Sea. There are others like them, but these two bodies of water are found in the country of Israel. The Sea of Galilee is much smaller and lies to the north. It receives water in and also generously gives water out through the Jordan River which flows south into the Dead Sea. The Sea of Galilee is full of fish and plants and provides food and life for many. On the other hand, the Dead Sea only takes and gives nothing back except salt. No fish or plant life can live there. If only the Dead Sea could give water out and become alive again. Remember, teach others and your progress will surprisingly improve.

3. <u>Sing Songs</u>: Singing songs has magic that no other exercise can duplicate. When you sing songs over and over again, you automatically memorize the words and phrases. When someone says, "Let's sing 'Jingle Bells' or 'Happy Birthday',

immediately you begin to sing the song exactly right without even thinking about it. There is no hesitation, no translation, no confusion. You just sing and enjoy. Also, while singing you are practicing saying words and, at the same time, practicing pronunciation because you verbalize each word more slowly and exactly with the music. That's what music can do for your ability to speak English. So choose good songs and good music with words you want to remember and be able to say. It is amazing how quickly you can learn to speak by singing. Finally, the Chinese language has many tones and in a way the language is sung. When you sing songs in English your brain can quickly connect the thoughts and meanings with sounds. Bingo – you speak!

4. Talk to the TV & Radio: There are English speaking television and radio channels. Find them and watch and listen to them, but more importantly, talk to them. This may seem strange and your family or friends may think you're crazy, but it is almost as effective as having a foreigner or native English speaker right in our room all the time. Listening is a great way to learn, but if you speak back and ask questions, then your mind and speaking mechanism benefits as if you were talking to a real person. True, the TV and radio will not answer your questions nor will they pause for your comments. Nevertheless, when you do this, your listening skills will improve and your ability to ask good questions and give good answers will also improve. Try it, you'll like it. You will need to work at it because we are in the habit of just listening to the radio and TV. Listening is good, but speaking is better. It makes all the difference.

5. Read Aloud & Read A Lot: Good teachers always emphasize the value of extensive reading. It's through reading many stories and books that one absorbs the culture, meaning and beauty of the language. So let me say here, "Read, read,

and read!" But in addition to just reading, read aloud. Little children learn to speak by listening to their mothers read to them. Mothers learn to read and speak better by reading and speaking to their children. Together, both the reader and listener learn to tell stories and add drama and emphasis to words and expressions. So read to others whenever you can. If there is no one to read to, then read aloud to yourself. Read aloud a lot!

6. <u>Call Others on the Telephone</u>: This can be one of the most common and most helpful methods of improving your spoken English. First, you must identify others who are willing to speak to you in English on the telephone. These can be your friends, classmates, workmates or family members. You can just call to surprise them or you can make appointments to speak to a number of people every day. At first, you may only speak for a few minutes, but as you improve you can spend more time on each call. The value comes in developing your ability to hear and understand the other person that you cannot see. You may need to repeat yourself or ask them to repeat what they have said or to speak more slowly. Soon, your ear will become accustomed and your speech will also improve so your calling partner can understand you better. This can be a fun and very useful practice that exercises many parts of your brain, ear and tongue.

7. <u>Group Participation</u>: Whether you are in a small group or attend a formal English class at a school, university or training company, it is vital that you participate. This means that you must ask questions, offer your opinions and actively contribute to the class or group's speaking activities. It's only when you become an active participant that your mind and mouth work together to speak and improve speaking. If you remain a passive spectator then

your left-brain will record what you see and hear while your right brain weakens and speaking difficulty increases. Also, remember that you cannot participate if you do not attend. Be an active and dedicated member of your group or class. As you participate, you are practicing many of the skills necessary to increase verbal speech.

8. Interpret For Others: Interpreting is one of the strongest methods of exercising your whole brain to improve your speaking ability. You are forced to draw on your left brain reserves while you exercise your right brain skills. It is similar to teaching others, but even more powerful because you are having to hear in Chinese, mentally understand and translate information in your mind and almost instantly verbalize these ideas correctly in English. The more advanced your English speaking ability is, the better interpreter you are. It only stands to reason that you should begin very early to interpret. Don't wait until you are proficient in speaking and then learn to interpret. Keep in mind that interpreting is not translating written documents. That is another very different skill involving mostly the left brain.

9. Memorize New Words & Phrases: In order to progress in learning to speak English, it is vital that you add new words to your vocabulary. Perhaps there are words assigned or those you desire to learn. It always helps to have a small list of words that you are referring to in order to master them. The only way you can truly master them is to use them in every day conversation. Only when you speak the words in sentences will you own them. If you faithfully do this over a period of a few years, your vocabulary will be as large as most native English speakers.

In addition to adding new vocabulary words, you add phrases, groups of words and entire sentences. When you begin adding phrases and whole sentences to your "vocabulary" and then use them in your speech, you are making great progress in your ability to speak English. Remember, don't just memorize them in your mind. Use them in your everyday speaking. Speak! Speak! Speak!

10. <u>Read, Write and Memorize Poetry</u>

"Words do not convey meaning, they call them forth."
- David O. McKay

"Poetry restores to words their power to evoke presence."
- Marcel

Like music, poetry enlightens the soul while it exercises the mind in rhythm and vivid imagery. By reading, writing and memorizing poetry, you are exercising one of the highest forms of spoken English. It energizes both the left and right brain while it conditions your thinking and trains your tongue.

So there you are, 10 easy exercises you can do on your own or with friends. It doesn't cost you a penny, only some time and consistent effort and dedication. If you measure your progress each day, each week and each month you will visually see your progress. Let me remind you again, you are only competing with yourself, so be honest in your evaluation and scoring.

Your Dreams Can Come True

Your dream to speak English fluently can and will come true. Just remember that where ever you are in your progress, your English is very good. Remind yourself that you are making excellent progress.

You have a responsibility to share what you have learned with others. Not just the ability to speak English, but the ability to teach others how to speak English. Is there room for improvement? Of course there is room for improvement. You can even improve on your spoken Chinese. Did you ever stop to realize that even your spoken Chinese is not perfect? That's OK. My spoken English is not perfect and I'm a native English speaker. I too am always trying to improve my spoken English. Perhaps you may even speak better English than I do, but maybe you don't believe it. Because you don't believe it, you don't have the confidence and you don't speak. That's a pity.

Believe me, your English is good and it's getting better. As you progress, your self-esteem will improve and confidence will grow. Soon, your ability to speak and express yourself will surprise you.

There will even come a time when you will begin to dream in English. Yes, dream in English. It's better than dreaming in color. When you dream in English you will know that you are making great progress in your spoken English. You will know that your dream to speak English very well is actually coming true.

Good luck to you! May all your dreams come true and may you speak English today and for ever after.

Review: Method of Recording & Scoring Your Results

These simple methods will remind you to do the activity, require you to keep a record of your progress and will show you where you are putting the most effort and where you need to improve. At the end of each day or week simply give an honest and objective evaluation of how you did during that day or week. Give yourself a number score from 0 to 10 in each activity area.

The numbers represent the following rating: 0 = no effort or failure to perform; 1 = very poor effort; 2 = little effort; 3 = not so good effort; 4 = below average; 5 = average; 6 = above average effort; 7 = very good effort; 8 = a lot of effort; 9 = excellent effort; 10 = perfect or maximum score available.

Add the total score for each day and then the total score for the whole week and/or month. You can follow your progress on the EASE Chart by plotting your cumulative average of your weekly scores. Just add up all the weekly scores and divide by the total number of weeks. That will give you your cumulative score. You may want to prepare your own spreadsheet in your computer to quickly and easily calculate and plot these scores. If you are not sure how to do it, you can ask a friend who is a computer expert.

10 Secrets - Scoring Chart
(Measure Your Progress)

Score: 0 = no effort or failure to perform; 1 = little effort; 2 = below average; 3 = average; 4 = good effort; 5 = excellent effort.

Day	C	TO	SS	TV	RA	ST	GP	IO	MW	RW	TT
1											
2											
3											
4											
5											
6											
7											
8											
9											
10											
11											
12											
13											
14											
15											
16											
17											
18											
19											
20											
21											
22											
23											
24											
25											
26											
27											
28											
29											
30											
31											

Legend: **C** = Confidence; **TO** = Teach Others; **SS** = Sing Songs; **TV** = Talk to the TV and/or Radio; **RA** = Read Aloud & Read a Lot; **ST** = Speak on Telephone; **GP** = Group Participation/Daily Dose (daily conversation program); **IO** = Interpret for Others; **MW** = Memorize Words and Phrases; **RW** = Read and Write Poetry; **TT** = Total Score.

流利使用英语的十条秘诀

Dale Christensen 著　2001年11月

前言

中国人学习英语已经很多年了，他们学习语法，词汇量也很大，但是在口语交流方面却有很大的困难。造成这种现象的原因是几个关键的障碍，这些障碍都是可以克服的。其中一个最大的障碍是恐惧心理。另一个障碍是学习者习惯于先在脑中将汉语翻译成英语，然后转化成口头的词语或者句子。这些问题都是由于中国人学习英语的方式引起的。

英语学习

<u>按照儿童学说话的方式学习语言。</u>理解并且会说一门语言是儿童必须逐步习得的一种基本技能。幼儿可以同时学习多门语言。他们会倾听一段时间，然后自己试着去重复。在通常情况下，他们处于较好的语言学习环境中，可以促进语言的学习。如果孩子们取得一点点成就或者进步，父母都会给予赞扬。因此，儿童就会鼓起勇气学习语言，并对此感到兴奋。请注意一点，在很长一段时间之后孩子们才开始学习有关语法、拼写和规则的句子结构。他们关注的是口语表达和交流。

<u>语言教师应该避免批评学生，应该尽量鼓励并赞扬他们。</u>如果某个学生懒于或者不愿意开口学习说一门新语言，激励他的最好方法是不要批评他，要赞许他的努力。频繁的批评或者挑错可能会让学生情绪沮丧，失去自信，对说语言产生恐惧心里。

学习说一门语言是右脑的一项活动。右脑还支配着其它多项活动，如艺术、音乐、运动能力、协调性、创造性和想象力。左脑支配着一些秩序性的活动，如记忆、数学、自然科学、逻辑思考、计算等活动。中国儿童在幼时运用右脑学习说汉语。然而，也许是因为学习中文需要记忆很多汉字，或者是因为其它原因，通常人们运用左脑学习和理解语言。

　　中国的教育体制促使学生采用左脑式学习。中国的教育制度和考试制度重视知识的记忆和学习自然科学，我们发现中国学生在上述领域内做得非常出色。可是，这些优秀的学生在学习英语语言方面有着很大的困难。他们最大的希望是能够说一口流利的英语，可这也是他们最担心的事情。大多数情况下，他们无法克服这种巨大的障碍和挑战。他们继续刻苦地学习语言知识，记忆大量的词汇和语法规则。

"哑巴"英语

　　有的学生非常刻苦地学习英语，可是经常无法运用所学的语言知识并开口将语言说出来，因此觉得苦恼。我们将这种语言称之为"哑巴语言"。他们会读会写，可是不会说。

目的

　　"流利使用英语的十条秘诀"这篇文章的目的是为了提高口语能力提供十条重要的原则、活动和方法。这些秘诀的最终目标是帮助学生学习英语并且流利地用英语交流。语言学习者拥有了各种学习的工具和技能，以及一个良好的学习环境，这样他们就可以克服恐惧心理，通过个人努力以及互相竞争不断地进步。

保证

如果能够正确运用并严格遵循这几条原则，就可以保证每个人能够大幅度地提高口语的流利度。你不再需要再依赖英语本族人来提高口语能力。是的，寻求英语本族人的协助会带来很大的好处，可是如果你遵循以下规则，你同样可以依靠自己提高口语能力。这一点是绝对保证的！

方法和评估

这些简单的方法会提醒你做一些活动，并且需要你记录下自己的进度，这将会让你明白你那些方面花了很大功夫，那些地方需要改进。在每天或者每星期结束的时候，要对你在这一天或者这一周内完成的事情做一个诚实并且客观的评估。在每项活动的评估中，用数字0至10来划分等级：0＝没有任何努力或者失败；1＝及其微小的努力；2＝努力了一点点；3＝不是很令人满意的努力；4＝略低于平均水平；5＝平均水平；6＝略高于平均水平；7＝不错的努力；8＝很多努力；9＝很优秀的成果；10＝能够达到的最高水准。

十条秘诀

1. <u>自尊</u>：拥有自尊心是学习说一门语言时最重要的一点。自尊心就是你对自己的感觉，包括心中的想法，或者自言自语时对自己说的"话"。对自己的感觉决定了心中所想，而心中的想法又决定了要说些什么和说话的方式。如果你对自己感觉良好，你就会说些好话，而且会以很和善的方式说话。如果对自己感觉很差，那么就会有一些负面的想法。当大多数的中国人被问及他们的英语程度的时候，或者有人赞扬他们的英语水平很好的时候，他们会立刻回答："哦，我的英语很差。我没有机会练习我的英语。"不要对你自己说这些话，也不要对别人这么说。如果你经常这么说，你自己就会慢慢开始相信事情确实如此，很快地，你的语言能力就会瘫痪，再也不会开口说英语了。你的右脑无法说出或者运用上你的左脑中贮存的知识，所以你会忘记你学到的知识。在学习说英语的过程中，必须丢掉中国人谦虚的传统。如果有人赞扬你，你只要说声"谢谢"。当有人问起你的英语程度或者批评你的时候，要这样礼貌地回答："我喜欢说英语。""我的英语有进步。"或者"我正在努力提高我的英语水平。"这些话语将加强你对自己的良好印象。随着信心的增强，你将会不再害怕，可以更加随意地说英语。你的大脑是世界上最奇妙的计算机。不要对自己或者别人说一些不好的想法而让大脑无法运转或者染上病毒。

2. <u>向别人教授知识</u>　　众所周知，教师比学生学到的东西要多。向别人传授东西的时候能够得到更多的东西。如果一个人总是接受别人的东西，他很快就会残废，会死去。首先，当你教别人说英语的时候，你会忘记自己的存在，集中精神帮助他人。这是学习中很重要的一段过程。当你给予的越多，实际上得到的越多。当你教导别人或者鼓励别人的时候，就会提高自己的语言能力。其次，当你教导别人的时候，你不得不运用自己所有的关于学习语言的知识。你必须记得贮存在左脑中的所有知识，并转移至右脑，从汉语翻成英语，然后必须转化成言语。如果要将某项知识教给别人，你必须说出来。你在教导、鼓励学生，或者纠正学生错误的时候，你听见自己的话语，因而能够了解自己的需求，并改正自己的错误。这是激励自己的一个很好的方法。

几千年以来，这个方法一直是学习的一个重大秘诀。这种方法同完全被动地接受知识的学习方法是不同的，为了比较出两者的差异，我们可以看看以下这个关于著名的加里海和死海的故事。有很多其它类似的海，可是这片水域都位于以色列境内。加里海比较小，位于北部。它接受外来的河水，同时也很慷慨地通过约旦河向外输送河水，约旦河向南流入死海。加里海中有很多鱼类和植物生存，给很多生物提供食物。而另一方面，死海却只是接受外来河水，提供出来的东西只有盐而已。鱼类和植物都无法在那里生存。如果死海能够向外排水，那就能够重新复活过来。记住，教导别人，你自己可能会有意想不到的进步。

3. <u>唱歌：</u>开口唱歌有很大的魔力，这是别的练习都无法与之相比的。当你一遍又一遍地高歌的时候，你会自然而然的记住单词和短语。当有人说道："让我们来唱'小铃铛'或者'祝你生日快乐'的时候，"，你立刻就会开始唱，甚至不用想都能唱得出来。你不会犹豫，不用翻译，也不会感到迷惑。只是很快乐地唱着歌。同样的，当你唱歌的时候，你是在练习语言，同时也是在练习发音，这是因为你跟着音乐将每个词更慢更准确地说了出来。这样音乐可以帮助你提高口语能力。所以，选择一些优秀的歌曲，一些你想记住歌词并能够说出来的歌曲。你会很惊奇地发现，通过唱歌能很快提高口语能力。最后，汉语有多种语调，从某种角度看来，说汉语就是把汉语"唱"出来。当你用英语唱歌的时候，你的脑子可以将思想和意义与发音联系起来。好了——你其实是开口说出来了。

4. <u>与电视或者收音机交谈</u>：有很多关于英语口语的电视和广播频道。要收听这些节目，可更重要的是要与它们交谈。这样做好像很奇怪，你的家人和朋友可能会认为你发疯了，可是这很有效，等于是房间里一直有一个英国人。依靠听来学习语言是一种很好的方法，可如果你对听到的内容有所回应，并提出问题，那么你的大脑和言语机制就会有很大的收益，就好像面对一个真人一样。当然，电视和广播不会回答你的问题，也不会停下了等待你的评论。然而，当你做这些事情的时候，你的听力会提高，同时也会提高你问问题和回答问题的能力。试一试这种做法，你会喜欢的。你需要努力做到这一点，因为我们一直都习惯于单纯地"听"广播和电视节目。练习听力是好的，但是能开口说点东西就更好了。这很重要。

5. <u>大声朗读和大量阅读：</u>优秀的教师总是强调泛读的重要性。通过阅读大量的故事和书籍才能理解一门语言的文化、内涵和它的优美之处。所以，我要说："读书，读书，再读书！"可是除了阅读书籍之外，还要大声朗读。幼儿通过听母亲朗读各种书籍来学习说话。通过读书给孩子听以及和孩子说话，母亲们会读得更好。这样，朗读者和听众都学会讲故事，而且让词语表达更加丰富。所以，尽量争取朗读书籍给别人听。如果没有人听，就对着自己大声朗读。要多多大声朗读！

6. <u>打电话给别人：</u>这种做法可能是提高英语口语最常用最有效的方法。首先，你要确定那些人可以与你在电话中用英语交谈，可以是朋友、同学、同事或者家人。每天你都可以突然打电话给他们，给他们一个惊喜，或者同某人约好通电话。刚开始的时候，你可以只说几分钟，当你的口语慢慢提高的时候，你可以多说一些。这可以帮助你提高在看不见对方的情况下的听力和理解力。你可能需要将某些话重复说几遍，也可能要请求对方重复或者说慢一些。很快地，你就会听习惯了，言语能力也会提高，电话的另一方也能更好地理解你的语言。这种练习很有趣，也很有用，可以训练你大脑、耳朵和舌头的多方功能。

7. <u>参加班级活动</u>：无论你是在一个小团体里学习英语或者是参加了学校或者培训公司的正式英语班级，加入集体活动是很重要的。这意味着你必须提出问题，表明观点，以及积极参与班级和团体的口语练习活动。只有当你积极参与活动的时候，你的大脑和嘴巴才能一起动起来，提高口语能力。如果你只做一个被动的观众，你的左脑会记录下你的所见所闻，而你的右脑会慢慢失去作用，渐渐会产生言语障碍。同样还要记住，如果不参加学习团体，就谈不上什么集体活动。当你参与活动的时候，你就在练习多项技能，这些技能都是提高语言能力必不可少的。

8. <u>替别人作口头翻译</u>：口译是训练整个大脑能力的最有效方法之一，可以提高你的口语能力。在训练右脑机能的同时，你必须利用左脑中储存的知识。这同教导别人的效果是类似的，却比之要更有效，这是因为你听到的是汉语，然后在脑中将这些信息译成英语，与此同时还要立刻用英语说出来。你的英语水平越高，你的口译能力越好。很早就要开始练习口译，不要一直等到你的口语很流利的时候才去学习口译。要记住口译不是翻译书面文件。笔译是另一种技能，主要与左脑有关。

9. <u>背诵一些句子和短语：</u>这项练习类似于增加新词汇，然而，除了增加单词之外，你还要多记忆整个句子。当你将句子和短语加入你的"词汇量"中，并且在言语中使用这些句子和短语的时候，你将会大大提高你的英语口语水平。记住，不要只是单纯地记住这些句子和短语，要在每天的日常言语中运用。要开口说英语！开口说！开口说！

10. <u>读、写、背诵诗歌</u>

"词语不能表达意思，他们会使意思丧失。
- David O. McKay

"诗歌能恢复词语产生风采的力量。
- Marcel

正如音乐一样，诗歌通过对大脑富有节奏、充满意境的训练启迪我们的智慧。在读、写、背诵诗歌的过程中，你实际上在操练最高水平的口语。这将改变你的思维，训练你的表达能力，将使左、右脑都充满活力。

好了，这就是十种简单的练习，你可以和自己做或者和朋友一起做。这些联系不需要花钱，只需要花时间，要坚持不懈，要认真去做。如果每天、每星期、每个月你都能够评估你自己的进度，你就会看到你的进步。让我再次提醒你，你只是在和自己比赛，所以，在评估的时候要诚实。

你会梦想成真

能流利说英语的梦想会成为现实。要记住，不论你进展情况如何，你的英语都是很棒的。经常告诉自己你正在取得很快的进步。

还需提高吗？当然需要。你甚至可以提高你的汉语口语。你是否没有意识到，你的汉语口语也并非完美。

不过这没关系，我的母语是英语，但是我的英语也不是完美的。我也总是在努力完善我的英语口语。也许有朝一日你的英语比我说得好，但是也许你不相信这一点。正是因为你不相信这一点，所以你没有自信，也就不开口说。这很遗憾。.

相信我，你的英语很好，而且正在不断进步。随着英语的不断完善，你的自信心也会相应增强。很快你的口语能力以及表达能力将会给你自己一个惊喜。

甚至从某一天开始，你在梦中都会用英语。是的，用英语做梦。这比用色彩做梦要好。当你用英语做梦时，你就会知道你的英语口语发面进步很快。而且逆流里说英语的梦想也会很快成真。

祝你好运！心往你梦想成真，今天快乐，永远快乐！

复习：纪录方法及打分方法

这些简单的方法将提醒你做各项活动，要求你记录下进展情况，而且可以显示你正将大部分精力在致力于哪些方面、以及那些方面有待改进。在周末或月末，只需客观、诚实地给自己在过去的一周或一个月中的表现做一个评估。在每项活动的空格里给自己打一个分（0—10分）

各分数代表以下等级：0＝没有任何努力或者失败；1＝及其微小的努力；2＝努力了一点点；3＝不是很令人满意的努力；4＝低于平均水平；5＝平均水平；6＝高于平均水平；7＝不错的努力；8＝非常努力；9＝很优秀的成果；10＝最高水准。

对每天的各项分数进行累计，然后累计得出各周分数的总和。然后把累计的和除以周数，这样你便可以有效的观察自己的进展情况。可利用EASE表格，将你每周平均分得累加结果用曲线图表示出来。你可以在计算机上用电子表格来快速计算、划出曲线图。如果你不知道应该怎样利用电子表格的话，那么就去请教计算机专家。

10 Secrets - Scoring Chart
(Measure Your Progress)

Score: 0 = no effort or failure to perform; 1 = little effort; 2 = below average; 3 = average; 4 = good effort; 5 = excellent effort.

Day	C	TO	SS	TV	RA	ST	GP	IO	MW	RW	TT
1											
2											
3											
4											
5											
6											
7											
8											
9											
10											
11											
12											
13											
14											
15											
16											
17											
18											
19											
20											
21											
22											
23											
24											
25											
26											
27											
28											
29											
30											
31											

Legend: **C** = Confidence; **TO** = Teach Others; **SS** = Sing Songs; **TV** = Talk to the TV and/or Radio; **RA** = Read Aloud & Read a Lot; **ST** = Speak on Telephone; **GP** = Group Participation/Daily Dose (daily conversation program); **IO** = Interpret for Others; **MW** = Memorize Words and Phrases; **RW** = Read and Write Poetry; **TT** = Total Score.

10 Secretos a Hablar Inglés

Información

Las personas Chinas estudian Inglés durante muchos años. Ellos aprenden la gramática y tienen un vocabulario muy bueno, pero ellos continúan tener dificultad a hablar. Hay varios obstáculos claves que causa que este fenómeno, que pueda es fácilmente y rápidamente vence. ¡Uno de los obstáculos más grandes es el temor! Otro obstáculo es la necesidad y el hábito para traducir mentalmente del Chino al Inglés y entonces convertir estos pensamientos en palabras y oraciones habladas. Muchas de estas dificultades son causadas por la manera personas Chinas estudian y aprenden el Idioma Inglés.

Aprender el Idioma

<u>Aprenda a hablar como un niño aprende a hablar</u>. Aprender a entender y hablar un idioma es uno de las primeras habilidades que un niño desarrolla. Los niños pequeños son capaces de aprender muchos idiomas al mismo tiempo. Ellos escuchan para un tiempo y entonces ellos tratan de repetir. Generalmente, su ambiente que aprende es muy amistoso y alentar. Los padres dan gran elogio para los esfuerzos más pequeños y mejoras más leves. Por lo tanto, el niño desarrolla el valor y se emociona acerca de aprender. Recuerde, es mucho tiempo antes ellos saben algo acerca de gramática, deletreando o la estructura formal de la oración. Su foco entero está a hablar y comunicar.

<u>Los maestros del idioma deben evitar la crítica y ser muy alentador y generoso con el elogio</u>. Si alguien es perezoso o

no quiere aprender a hablar un idioma nuevo, la mejor manera de motivarlos los deberán alabar para sus esfuerzos y nunca criticar. La crítica o indicando los defectos con demasiada frecuencia causan que el estudiante esté inquieto y ellos pierden confianza en sí mismo y desarrollan el temor de hablar.

Aprender a hablar cualquier idioma es una actividad correcta de cerebro. Otras actividades o calidades del cerebro-derecho o calidades incluyen el movimiento y coordinación físicos, el arte, la música, la creatividad y la imaginación. El lado izquierdo del cerebro domina las cosas muy ordenadas y estructuradas como la memorización, las matemáticas, la ciencia, el pensamiento lógico, dando cuenta etc. Los niños Chinos jóvenes aprenden a hablar Chino que utilizando el lado cerebro-derecho. Pero quizás porque el idioma Chino requiere mucha memorización de etc. Chino de caracteres la ciencia del idioma se aprende o es entendida en una manera muy izquierda de cerebro.

El sistema de enseñanza Chino promueve el desarrollo izquierdo de cerebro. A causa de la muy naturaleza del sistema de enseñanza Chino foco de s a aprender información, memorizando, el foco científico y su probar y los métodos de adelantamiento, nosotros encontramos que estudiantes Chinos sobresalen en estas áreas. Sin embargo, estos mismos estudiantes tienen gran dificultad en su capaz de hablar o de otro modo para expresar con palabras el idioma Inglés. Su deseo más grande deberá hablar Inglés con soltura, pero esto es también su temor más grande. La mayoría de las veces, es un obstáculo o desafía demasiado grande para muchos en vencer. Ellos continúan estudiar diligentemente la ciencia del idioma y desarrollar un vocabulario y la comprensión grandes de etc. de reglas de gramática.

El Idioma "Mudo"

Los estudiantes más diligentes del idioma Inglés a menudo son frustrados porque ellos no acaban de poder parece conseguir acceso a su conocimiento y lo obtiene fuera de su boca. Para esta razón, muchos de ellos lo llaman un "mudo" el idioma. ¡Ellos lo entienden y pueden leer y lo puede escribir, pero ellos no lo pueden hablar!

El Propósito

El propósito de los *10 Secretos de Hablar Ingles* deberá proporcionar los principios claves, las actividades y los métodos de la medida que todos pueden utilizar para mejorar su habilidad parlante. La meta de estos secretos deberá ayudar a personas gozan aprender y comunicando con soltura en Inglés. Los oradores ahora pueden tener los instrumentos y las habilidades junto con un ambiente amistoso donde ellos pueden vencer sus temores, gozar y medir su progreso por el esfuerzo y/o la competencia personales con otros.

La Garantía

Si utilizado correctamente y seguido diligentemente, cada participante es garantizado que su fluidez parlante no sólo aumentará dramáticamente, pero acelerará. Usted no necesita un extranjero ni a orador Inglés nativo mejorar su habló Inglés. Sí, eso sería una ventaja maravillosa, pero usted puede mejorar dramáticamente en su propio siguiendo estas pautas. ¡Eso's una promesa y una garantía!

El Método & Rayando

Estos métodos sencillos lo recordarán para hacer la actividad, requiéralo llevar un registro de su progreso y mostrar usted donde usted ponen las la mayoría de los esfuerzos y de donde usted necesita mejorar. A finales de cada día o semana dan simplemente una evaluación honesta y objetiva de cómo usted hizo durante ese día o la semana. Dese una cuenta del número de 0 a 10 en cada área del actividad. Los números representan la calificación de siguiente: 0 = no esfuerzo ni el fracaso para realizar; 1 = el esfuerzo muy pobre; 2 = el esfuerzo pequeño; 3 = el esfuerzo no tan bueno; 4 = peor que el común; 5 = promedia; 6 = el esfuerzo por encima de lo mediano; 7 = el esfuerzo muy bueno; 8 = mucho esfuerzo; 9 = el esfuerzo excelente; 10 = perfecciona o el máximo raya disponible.

10 Secretos

1. Amor propio: El aspecto más importante de hablar tiene amor propio bueno. Amor propio es cómo usted se siente acerca de usted mismo. Incluye cómo usted piensa y lo que usted dice a usted mismo o "auto discurso". Qué usted se siente determina lo que usted piensa y lo que usted piensa determina lo que usted dice y cómo usted lo dice. Si usted se siente bueno acerca de usted mismo, usted dirá las cosas buenas y hablará bien. Si usted se siente las cosas malas acerca de usted mismo, ted pensará los pensamientos negativos. Usted no tendrá confianza en sí mismo. En lugar usted tenusdrá el temor y usted no hablará. Cuándo la mayoría de las personas Chinas son preguntadas cómo su Inglés es o si ellos son dichos el heredero Inglés es muy bueno, ellos responden inmediatamente diciendo, "Ah, mi Inglés es muy pobre. Tengo ninguna oportunidad de practicar." Dice no esto a usted mismo y no lo dice a otros. Si usted lo dice a menudo suficiente, usted empezará a creerlo y pronto usted será paralizado e incapaz de hablar. Usted empezará a olvidarse lo que usted sabe porque el cerebro correcto no puede hablar ni puede utilizar el conocimiento que usted ha almacenado en el cerebro izquierdo. A aprender a hablar Inglés, usted debe poner la costumbre China de modestia o humildad aparte. Cuándo alguien lo cumplimenta, dice

apenas gracias. Si alguien pregunta cómo su Inglés es o lo critica, responde en una manera positiva diciendo algo como, "adoro hablar Inglés." O "Mi Inglés mejora." O "trabajo muy duro mejorar mi Inglés." Estas declaraciones positivas reforzarán los pensamientos positivos y los sentimientos buenos. Con la confianza aumentada, usted vencerá el temor y hablará más libremente. Su mente es la computadora más fantástica en el universo. Póngase lo quita o le da virus mortales diciendo o piensa las cosas negativas a usted mismo o a otros.

2. <u>Enseñe los Otros</u>: Es un hecho conocido que el maestro aprende más que el estudiante. Uno recibe más cuando ellos dan. Cuándo una persona sólo recibe ellos llegan a ser paralizados y pronto mueren. Ante todo, cuando usted enseña otra persona para hablar Inglés usted se olvida y el concentrado en porción otra persona. Esto es un proceso clave a aprender. Usted obtiene verdaderamente más cuando usted da más. Usted se mejora en hablar cuando usted da los otros las instrucciones y el ánimo. En segundo lugar, cuando usted enseña usted es forzado a utilizar todas las habilidades de hablar bien. Usted debe recordar lo que usted ha almacenado en el cerebro izquierdo, lo transfiere a la derecha lado, lo traduce de Chino (Español) al Inglés y entonces usted es forzado a expresar con **palabras**. Usted lo debe hablar para enseñarlo. Usted se oye habla y puede reconocer sus propias necesidades y se corrige mientras usted enseña, corrige y **adelenta** a su estudiante (s). 'S un gran método y un proceso que auto motivando.

Durante millares de años, este método ha sido un secreto poderoso a aprender. Para comparar la diferencia a recibir apenas y tomando para aprender que podemos utilizar el cuento dicho acerca de dos famosos mares, el Mar de Galilea y el Mar Muerto. Hay los otros como ellos, pero estas dos masas de agua se encuentran en el país de Israel. El Mar de Galilea es mucho más pequeño y las mentiras al norte. Recibe agua en y también da generosamente agua fuera por el Río de Jordania que fluye al sur en el Mar Muerto. El Mar de Galilea está repleto de pez y plantas y proporciona alimento y vida para muchos. Por otro lado, el Mar Muerto sólo toma y no da nada apoya menos sal. Ninguna vida del pez ni la planta puede vivir allí. Si solamente el Mar Muerto podría dar agua fuera y llegar a ser vivo otra vez. Recuerde, enseñe los otros y su progreso mejorarán sorprendentemente.

3. <u>Cante las Canciones</u>: Cantando las canciones tienen la magia que ningún otro ejercicio puede duplicar. Cuándo usted canta las canciones repetidamente otra vez, usted memoriza automáticamente las palabras y las frases. Cuándo alguien dice, "Permitió canta 'las Campanas de Retintín' o 'los Cumpleaños Felices', inmediatamente usted empieza a cantar la canción exactamente correcto sin pensando aún acerca de lo. No hay la vacilación, ninguna traducción, ninguna confusión. Usted acaba de cantar y goza. También, al cantar usted practica palabras de dicho y, al mismo tiempo, practicando la pronunciación porque usted expresa con palabras cada palabra más lentamente y exactamente con la música. Eso lo que música puede hacer para su habilidad de hablar Inglés. Así que escoge las canciones buenas y la música buena con palabras que usted quiere recordar y ser capaz de decir. Asomba cuán rápidamente usted puede aprender a hablar cantando. Finalmente, el idioma Chino tiene muchos tonos y de una manera el idioma se canta. Cuándo usted canta las canciones en Inglés su cerebro puede conectar rápidamente los pensamientos y medios con sonidos. ¡Bingo (instante) – usted habla!

4. <u>Hable a la Televisión & la Radio</u>: Hay hablar Inglés la televisión y los canales de la radio. Encuéntrelos y el reloj y los escucha, pero lo que es más importante, habla con ellos. Esto puede parecer extraño y su familia o los amigos pueden pensar Usted esta loco, pero es casi tan efectivo como tener un extranjero o el derecho Inglés nativo de orador en nuestro cuarto todo el tiempo. Escuchar es una gran manera de aprender, pero si usted habla espalda y hace preguntas, entonces su mente y beneficios parlantes de mecanismo como si sean una persona verdadera. Verdadero, la televisión y la radio no contestarán sus preguntas ni harán ellos se detienen para sus comentarios. No obstante, cuando usted hace esto, sus habilidades que escuchan mejorarán y su habilidad de hacer preguntas buenas y dar las respuestas buenas mejorarán también. Trátelo, usted como lo. Usted necesitará trabajar en lo porque solemos apenas "escuchando" a la radio y la televisión. Escuchar es bueno, pero hablar es mejor. Hace toda la diferencia.

5. <u>Lea en Voz Alta & Lee Mucho</u>: Maestros buenos siempre acentúan el valor de la lectura extensa. 'S por la lectura muchos cuentos y los libros que uno absorbe la cultura, significando y la belleza del idioma. Así que permitió que mí diga aquí, "Leyó, leyó, y leyó!" Pero además de leer apenas, para leer en voz alta. Los niños pequeños aprenden a hablar escuchando a sus madres leen a ellos. Las madres aprenden a leer y hablar mejor leyendo y hablando con sus niños. Juntos, el lector y oyente aprenden a decir los cuentos y agregar el drama y el énfasis a palabras y expresiones. Así que leyó a otros siempre que usted puede. Si hay nadie leer a, entonces leyó en voz alta a usted mismo. ¡Lea en voz alta mucho!

6. <u>Llame los Otros Por Teléfono</u>: Esto puede ser uno del muy común y la mayoría de los métodos útiles de mejorar

su habló Inglés. Primero, usted debe identificar los otros que están dispuestos a hablar con usted en Inglés en el teléfono. Estos pueden ser sus amigos, los compañeros de clase, miembros de colegas o familia. Usted acaba de llamar a sorprenderlos o usted puede hacer las citas para hablar con varias personas cada día. Al principio, usted puede sólo habla durante unos pocos minutos, pero cuando usted lo mejora puede dedicar más tiempo en cada llamada. El valor entra desarrollando su habilidad de oír y entender a la otra persona que usted no puede ver. Usted puede necesitar repetirse o pedir ellos repetir lo que ellos han dicho o para hablar más lentamente. Pronto, la oreja se acostumbrará y su discurso mejorará también tan su socio de llamamiento lo puede entender mejor. Esto puede ser una diversión y la práctica muy útil que ejercita muchas partes del cerebro, la oreja y la lengua.

7. <u>Agrupe la Participación</u>: Si usted está en un grupo pequeño o asiste una clase Inglesa formal en una escuela, la compañía de la universidad o la instrucción, es esencial que usted participe. Esto significa que usted debe hacer preguntas, ofrecer sus opiniones y contribuir activamente a la clase o el grupos que habla las actividades. 'S sólo cuando usted llega a ser un participante activo que su mente y boca trabajan juntos para hablar y mejorar hablar. Si usted se queda un espectador pasivo entonces su cerebro izquierdo registrará lo que usted ve y oye mientras el cerebro correcto debilita y los aumentos parlantes de dificultad. También, recuerda que usted no puede participar si usted no asiste. Sea un miembro activo y dedicado de su grupo o la clase. Cuando usted participa, usted practica muchas de las habilidades necesarias para aumentar discurso verbal.

8. <u>Interprete Para Otros</u>: Interpretar es uno de los métodos más fuertes de ejercitar el cerebro entero de mejorar su

habilidad parlante. Usted es forzado a utilizar sus reservas izquierdas de cerebro mientras usted ejercita sus habilidades correctas de cerebro. Es semejante a otros docentes, pero aún más poderoso porque usted tiene que oír en el Chino, entender mentalmente y traducir información en su mente y casi expresar con palabras instantáneamente estas ideas correctamente en Inglés. El más avanzó su Inglés que habla la habilidad es, el mejor intérprete que usted es. Sólo se para razonar que usted empieza muy interpretar temprano. Póngase la espera T hasta que usted sea capaz en hablar y entonces aprenda a interpretar. Tenga presente ese interpretar no traduce documentos escritos. Eso es otro implicar muy diferente de la habilidad en su mayor parte el cerebro izquierdo.

9. <u>Memorice Palabras Nuevas & las Frases</u>: Para el progreso a aprender a hablar Inglés, es esencial que usted agregue palabras nuevas a su vocabulario. Hay quizás palabras asignadas o esos usted desea de aprender. Siempre ayuda a tener una lista pequeña de palabras que usted se refiere a para los domina. La única manera que usted sinceramente los puede dominar los deberán utilizar en cada conversación de día. Sólo cuando usted habla las palabras en oraciones lo hacen los posee. Si usted hace fielmente esto sobre un período de unos pocos años, su vocabulario será tan grande como oradores Ingleses muy nativos. Este ejercicio es semejante a agregar palabras nuevas de vocabulario, pero en vez de apenas palabras, usted agrega las oraciones enteras. Cuándo usted empieza las citas que agregan y las frases a su "el vocabulario" y entonces los utiliza en su discurso, usted hace gran progreso en su habilidad de hablar Inglés. Recuerde, no solo apenas los memoriza en su mente. Utilícelos en su hablar diario. ¡Hable! ¡Hable! ¡Hable!

10. Lea, Escriba y Memorice la Poesía

"Palabras no transmiten el significado, ellos los llaman adelante."
- David O. McKay

"La Poesía restaura a palabras que su poder de provocar la presencia."
- Marcel

Como la música, la poesía aclara el alma mientras ejercita la mente en el ritmo e imágenes vívidas. Leyendo, escribir y memorizar la poesía su ejercitan uno de las formas más altas de habló Inglés. Vigoriza el cerebro de izquierda y derecho mientras condiciona su pensamiento y la instrucción de la lengua.

Así que allí usted es, 10 ejercicios fáciles que usted puede hacer en su propio o con amigos. No le costo un centavo, sólo algún tiempo y el esfuerzo y la dedicación constantes. Si usted mide su progreso cada día, cada semana y cada mes usted verá visualmente su progreso. Permita que mí lo recuerde otra vez, usted es sólo compitiendo con usted mismo, así que es honesto en su evaluación y rayar.

Sus Sueños Pueden Realizarse

Su sueño para hablar Inglés puede con soltura y se realizará. Recuerde apenas que dondequiera usted está en su progreso, su Inglés es muy bueno. Recuérdese que usted hace el progreso excelente.

Usted tiene una responsabilidad de compartir lo que ellos habían aprendido con otros. No apenas la habilidad de hablar Inglés, pero la habilidad de enseñar los otros a cómo hablar Inglés. ¿Hay el espacio para la mejora? Por supuesto hay el espacio para la mejora. Usted puede mejora aún en su Chino hablado. ¿Paró jamás usted darse cuenta de que aún su Chino hablado no es perfecto? Eso es BUENO. Mi habló Inglés no es perfecto y yo soy un orador Inglés nativo. Yo también siempre trato de mejorar mi habló Inglés. Quizás usted puede habla aún mejor Inglés que hago, pero quizá usted se pone lo cree. Y, porque usted se pone lo cree, usted se pone tiene la confianza y usted se pone habla. Eso es lástima.

Créame, su Inglés es bueno y's que mejorándose. Cuando usted progreso, su amor propio mejorará y la confianza crecerá. Pronto, su habilidad de hablar y expresarse lo sorprenderá.

Allí haga viene aún un tiempo cuando usted empezará a soñar en Inglés. Sí, el sueño en Inglés. 'S mejor que soñando en colores. Cuándo usted sueña en Inglés que usted sabrá que usted hace gran progreso en su habló Inglés. Usted sabrá que su sueño para hablar Inglés muy bien se realiza verdaderamente.

¡La buena suerte a usted! Pueda todos sus sueños se realizan y lo pueden vive felizmente hoy y para jamás después. Te quiero y yo tengo la confianza en usted. El adiós para ahora.

La revisión: el Método de Grabación & Rayando Sus Resultados

Estos métodos sencillos lo recordarán para hacer la actividad, requiéralo llevar un registro de su progreso y mostrar usted donde usted ponen las la mayoría de los esfuerzos y de donde usted necesita mejorar. A finales de cada día o semana dan simplemente una evaluación honesta y objetiva de cómo usted hizo durante ese día o la semana. Dese una cuenta del número de 0 a 10 en cada área del actividad. Los números representan la calificación de siguiente: 0 = no esfuerzo ni el fracaso para realizar; 1 = el esfuerzo muy pobre; 2 = el esfuerzo pequeño; 3 = el esfuerzo no tan bueno; 4 = peor que el común; 5 = promedia; 6 = el esfuerzo por encima de lo mediano; 7 =

el esfuerzo muy bueno; 8 = mucho esfuerzo; 9 = el esfuerzo excelente; 10 = perfecciona o el máximo raya disponible.

Agregue la cuenta total por cada día y entonces la cuenta total por la semana entera. Usted puede seguir su progreso en el Gráfico tramando su promedio cumulativo de sus cuentas semanales. Sume apenas todas las cuentas semanales y divida por el número total de semanas. Eso le dará su cuenta cumulativa. Usted puede querer también preparar su propia hoja de cálculo en su computadora a calcula fácilmente y rápidamente y trama estas cuentas. Si usted no está seguro cómo hacerlo, usted puede pedir a un amigo que es un experto de la computadora.

10 Secrets - Scoring Chart
(Measure Your Progress)

Score: 0 = no effort or failure to perform; 1 = little effort; 2 = below average; 3 = average; 4 = good effort; 5 = excellent effort.

Day	C	TO	SS	TV	RA	ST	GP	IO	MW	RW	TT
1											
2											
3											
4											
5											
6											
7											
8											
9											
10											
11											
12											
13											
14											
15											
16											
17											
18											
19											
20											
21											
22											
23											
24											
25											
26											
27											
28											
29											
30											
31											

Legend: **C** = Confidence; **TO** = Teach Others; **SS** = Sing Songs; **TV** = Talk to the TV and/or Radio; **RA** = Read Aloud & Read a Lot; **ST** = Speak on Telephone; **GP** = Group Participation/Daily Dose (daily conversation program); **IO** = Interpret for Others; **MW** = Memorize Words and Phrases; **RW** = Read and Write Poetry; **TT** = Total Score.

Teacher's Manual

Prelude to Fluency

Go Check It Out

Two months had passed since I had left the company I worked with for the previous two years, taking a new construction technology to China. I had visited China enough times to know that things were quite different than many of my American friends imagined. My wife and family had hoped to live in China for at least six months while working for this company just to have the experience. But, the investors who had purchased the company were not the kind of people I wanted to work with. So, I wanted to explore alternatives. One of my business contacts suggested that I go to China and explore possibilities there.

"Perhaps you will be able to find something from here or even teach at USTC as a visiting professor," Lu Wei wrote in his e-mail. "Meanwhile, you can give some lectures to our MBA students at the university. USTC (The University of Science & Technology of China) is considered to be one of the best schools in China. Because of their superiority in science and technology, it is referred to as the MIT or Cal Tech of China." After a considerable number of e-mail messages, it was agreed that the best way to explore future opportunities with the university and elsewhere was to go to Hefei and speak to the university and prospective employers face to face.

"Mary-Jo," I told my wife, "A month is a long time. But we can e-mail each other every day, and I will definitely be back before

Sam leaves for his two-year mission in Peru. You and Tamara will have to be ready to go shortly after the middle of January. I know that I'm going to like it. Are you OK with that?" Mary-Jo answered, "As long as I can be with you, I'll go anywhere."

I paused and waved a last farewell and went through the boarding gate to begin my long journey of adventure to a mystical land so far away. Mary-Jo waved one more time and then went to a window to watch the plane until it took off. She didn't leave until it was long out of sight above the clouds.

USTC MBA Program

Tamara got permission from Mountain View High School in Orem, Utah to graduate early so she could share the China experience with her parents. After arriving in Hefei, we stayed in the USTC Foreign Guest House and ate in the student cafeteria for two months while our apartment was being renovated. This was just the way it was supposed to be, and we loved every minute.

So many people befriended us. We were hosted at many dinners and invited to many special functions. The Vice Mayor and his wife, Linda, and son, John, became dear friends and we enjoyed many delicious meals at the invitation of Xu Hua, the owner of the Jin Man Lou restaurant chain. We all loved to dine with others, but I especially enjoyed having people ask me if I liked Chinese food. To this common question I would always answer, "Chinese food is my second most favorite thing I like about China." To which almost everyone would quickly ask, "What is your most favorite thing?" Then I would quickly smile and say with a wink or a twinkle in my eye, "The Chinese people of course!" This was always met with words of agreement in both Chinese and English and lots of raised glasses and toasts to good friends.

Tamara made friends with high school students her own age whom she met on campus. She also enrolled in my MBA classes and made many friends there. We recorded books together, were interviewed for TV and radio programs, and traveled to many beautiful places around China. This first semester was a wonderful experience for everyone.

However, there was one looming problem that just didn't seem to get any better. Even though our Chinese hosts complimented us on their progress, we all quietly complained to each other that the only problem was that it just seemed so difficult to learn to speak Chinese. Every day, five days a week, we took traditional Chinese classes for reading, writing and speaking. Each class had its own textbook and special teacher. Additionally, we had several very helpful tutors who were willing to come to our apartment and teach us privately. We couldn't have had it better, but still the fluency in speaking Chinese didn't seem to come as quickly as we had hoped.

The summer holiday went by quickly and soon the fall semester was beginning. Tamara had enrolled at BYU-Idaho and I again taught entrepreneurship and management communication along with a special lecture series on "Teaching Improvement". An international business class would be added to my schedule the following semester. Also, before leaving in the spring, Mary-Jo signed a year long contract to teach oral English at Ke Da (USTC). After the first week of classes, she felt overwhelmed by the magnitude of her new assignment.

"I just don't know how I'm going to be able to teach all 600 students how to speak English. Some of them only have classes once a week, others every other week. How can I teach them to speak English in such a short time?" she said in a pleading voice. She was not one to give in, but the challenge seemed almost insurmountable.

The Revelation – The Big Ah ha!!!

Late into the fall semester, I decided not to attend any more Chinese classes. They just weren't working for me. It was very obvious by that time that one of the reasons I wasn't learning to speak Chinese better was the same reason that the Chinese students weren't able to speak English. A lot of study and practice was required to understand the formal rules, tones, vocabulary words and characters. But there was little focus on learning how to speak Chinese. In fact, there were very few exercises in speaking at all. When I told the teachers that I didn't care about learning to read characters and only wanted to speak Chinese, they reminded me that characters and strokes were an important part of this ancient language and should be given their due attention. It was obvious to me that the traditional way of learning to speak a new language was not working for me.

Well, that was it. By now, I had seen hundreds of students who had been studying English for many years, and still they couldn't speak the language. Why? Was it because they didn't do their homework or perhaps they didn't really want to learn? Were they lazy or just plain stupid? No, these could not be the reasons. Many people studied English for 10 or 15 years and could read and write beautifully using excellent grammar. I had told many of them that they seemed to have a bigger vocabulary than mine. One day, it dawned on me that if they were intelligent and hard working, which they were, then the only rational conclusion could be that they were not being taught the right way.

Change The System – Find A Better Way

Could it be? That's it! "How could I have overlooked it for so long?" I asked at our dinner table. "It's the method of teaching that's all wrong, not the students. They are learning the English language all upside down!"

"OK, could you pass the rice and get another carton of milk out of the fridge?" asked Mary-Jo in a very matter of fact and uninterested tone.

In an effort to rally her support, I quickly followed her instructions and continued with even greater enthusiasm and emphasis, "Honey, don't you realize, instead of learning the English language the way they should, these people are being taught it all backwards? They should first learn how to hear and understand the language, then speak it before they are taught the scientific stuff".

"What do you mean, scientific stuff?" Mary-Jo quickly asked.

"You know, the rules and all the other dull boring stuff about grammar and conjugation. Hey, I didn't even start to learn that about English until I was almost in high school. When I was a baby, I listened until I started speaking. In the first grade I started to learn to spell and then read basic stuff. I had been speaking for years before I even knew what a word or sentence was let alone what correct spelling or grammar was."

Mary-Jo looked me square in the eye, "Well, what are you going to do about it, change the whole system?"

With this new understanding and that soft challenge from my sweetheart, I said, "Yeah, that's exactly what I'm going to do. I'm going to change the way people learn to speak English".

In undergraduate school at Boston College, I had majored in Biology and minored in Chemistry. So I was familiar with experimentation and taking a scientific approach. However, it was my business training and creativity that caused me to look at things in a different light. I had taught hundreds of students about the concept of TQM (total quality management) and how to always improve on things. It had become second nature to me. Learning to speak English the traditional way wasn't working. The challenge was to find a better way.

The Big Question

A few days later, I was walking from class to my apartment. As I walked across the courtyard in front of the Foreign Housing Building, two students introduced themselves and asked if I would consider teaching English at a company in town. They promised 100 Yuan per hour with no preparation. "All you need to do is show up and talk to the people and answer their questions," said one young man. I responded by saying that I was not an English teacher, but would keep it in mind. Somehow, in an effort to be on my way, I had given them my telephone number and within hours I received a call from Christina Li, the owner of the immigration company called CanaWin. "I need a native speaker for my clients," she repeated several times after I had explained that my minimum fee was 200 Yuan and I wasn't really interested.

"I would at least like to meet you. Won't you come to my office?" Christina coaxed.

"Ok, I'll try to come just to see what you are doing and have a look around. Maybe I can just observe for a few minutes," I agreed.

"Good," the next class is tomorrow from 2:00 to 4:00 p.m. I'd like to meet you then." Christina sounded very determined. We exchanged good-byes.

It was in this class that I heard the same question that so many of my MBA students had asked. It was the same question that Mary-Jo's students also asked me when I visited her classes to introduce myself. It was the question or comment that most Chinese business acquaintances made at some point in our conversations. Now in Christina's class, after he had offered a comment about the students getting settled in Canada and while I was in the middle of writing something on the whiteboard, the instructor quietly excused himself for a few minutes. "Does everyone understand?" Yes, everyone understood. "Well, are there any other questions?" I asked. Then it happened. I heard that same familiar question, "What is the secret to improving my spoken English?"

Almost in a knee jerk reaction and trying to be funny with a quick comeback, I said, "There is a secret to being fluent in speaking English. As a matter of fact, I know several secrets. I call them the *Seven Secrets*. They not only will improve your spoken English, but if you know these secrets and use them every day, your improvement will actually accelerate."

I then drew a graph on the board with a line showing steady improvement and then a second line curving upward showing dramatic accelerated improvement. Everyone almost gasped at the realization that there was someone who had the answer to their question and he was right in the same room.

"Please tell us!" they all pleaded in unison. "What are the *Seven Secrets*?"

"How badly do you want to know them? - How badly do you want to speak English?" I taunted.

"We want them very badly." "We will do anything to know them." "Please tell us!"

"OK, but before I tell you the *Seven Secrets*, I have two questions for you. The first question is, 'How much are you willing to pay me for them?'" I said this with a big grin on my face. For a brief moment, everyone silently stared back at me and then almost as if they had practiced their response, they all began to negotiate and ask how much was required. I continued to laugh as the noise subsided and silence again filled the room.

Then one woman in the back of the room asked, "What is your second question?" That's when I leaned very far forward with both hands on the table, and said almost in a whisper, "If I tell you, can you keep it a secret? I mean you can't tell anyone!" Startled by my answer, the room erupted in laughter and quick assurances that they wouldn't be shared with anyone.

When everyone regained their composure, I began to explain how people learn to speak their native language as a child. To help do this, I told how the brain is made up of the left and right sides and described what each side does and how they work together. Then I reviewed how a child begins to learn in school, first about the alphabet or characters and words, then sentences and language rules, etc. Yes, this was exactly how they had learned to speak Chinese. I continued to describe how they had then begun to learn this foreign language called English. Instead of first learning how to speak and then to read and write, they had studied the technical aspects for many years, but never mastered the practical application of speaking. Everyone agreed that this had been his or her experience exactly.

I began to share the secrets one by one. The students all agreed that the Chinese educational system emphasized examinations and the only practical examination was a written examination. Few or no oral examinations had ever been developed or used. The focus of their studies and efforts on vocabulary, memorization and visually being able to read and write. In addition, the cultural aspects and customs of students and teachers in the classroom made it seem almost impossible to verbalize anything beyond single words or memorized expressions.

No Criticism!

In a challenging tone, I asked, "How many of you hesitate to speak with others because you are afraid you'll make a mistake? How many of you feel that you cannot or should not speak until you can do it correctly?" Many heads were nodding as if to agree with what I was suggesting. I continued, "Have you ever had a teacher strongly correct you or maybe even criticize you if you make a mistake?" Again, the same nods of their heads. "How many of you have made a mistake or seen a classmate make a mistake and then everyone laughed?" Eyes began to look down and the heads seemed to nod more slowly as if to say, "You are right on target. How did you know that's what happens?" And, "How did you know that we feel very badly. No one wants to make a mistake and get laughed at."

Bull's-eye! I had hit the nail right on the head. Not only was the system of teaching English backwards and upside down, but also the Chinese culture and education methods were compounding the problem. There had to be a simpler way. There must be a way to quickly learn to speak and develop confidence in speaking so that learning the other aspects of the language can help the speaker to progress further, faster and correctly. "Is there a way?" I asked. "Yes there is! You now have it and if you follow these secrets and speak English every day, your life will never be the same!"

The English Class

Request From The Tibetan Students

During the following weeks, I spoke to many groups of people including high schools, college classes, seminars for companies and even special events. I always took advantage of the opportunity to share the Seven Secrets and encouraged the audiences to somehow keep track of their progress. Measuring their progress in speaking English was a vital ingredient to their success. Because there was no model for keeping track of such progress, I developed a chart and a scoring system. I soon discovered that it was awkward to score only *Seven Secrets* and there surely must be some other exercises to actually force people to speak. It dawned on me that Secrets 8, 9 and 10 had helped me as a teenager to gain confidence and to begin to verbalize my feelings and speak English in sentences that my parents and teachers could understand. If they helped me, then why not Chinese students trying learn to speak English?

At the time I was developing my *Seven Secrets* into my *10 Secrets To Accelerated English Fluency* booklet for edit and printing to be used as a study guide for my students or anyone else who wanted to improve their spoken English. My good friend Jane, an English master's degree student, called to ask me for help. "There is a group of Tibetan students at USTC who want to know if you would be their English teacher," she told me.

"Why do they want me? Why can't you teach them?" I queried.

"They want to have a native speaker and I will be there to help you," she reassured me for the third time.

"OK, I'll meet with them, but I can't promise anything."

The next evening, at exactly 7:00 p.m., there was a knock at my door. I ushered in Jane, Philip and Cari. They were a little older than I had expected, but they seemed like nice enough people. Jane had to interpret everything for everybody. Both parties only understood a few words of what the other was saying. It was obvious from the start that Jane would be a vital part of getting any kind of class started. She explained that their native language was Tibetan, and they had learned Chinese as a second language. They now wanted to learn English. I could see that there were even difficulties in the flow of communications between Jane and the two men, even though they all seemed to finally understand each other.

After the customary introductions were over and the explanation of the purpose of their visit had been explained, they asked Jane in Chinese how much I would charge for my services. She interpreted and my response: "How much are you willing to pay me?" It took a little coaxing and explanation for Jane to relay the question with the same directness that I wanted. This question seemed to confuse them, or at least it seemed like they hadn't expected it. For over five minutes they vigorously chattered back and forth with each other in Tibetan and then finally turned to Jane with their reply.

She explained, "They don't have a budget, so whatever they pay you will come out of their own pockets."

"I don't care where the money comes from, I want to know how badly they want to learn English," I insisted. "How much are they willing to pay?"

"They said they could pay you 70 Yuan per hour for three hours a week. They would like to meet more than once a week if it is possible. They seem to like you and want you to be their teacher." Jane continued.

I leaned forward and very intently instructed her in her next interpretation, "OK, now I want you to interpret exactly what I say to you. Is that clear?" I continued, "Tell them that I am a businessman and a visiting professor teaching MBA students how to do business. I am not an English teacher. I do not teach people English. I don't even want to teach English! But, if they want to learn to speak English, I can help them do that quickly, and they will surprise themselves with how fast they improve. Now tell them that."

She obediently and very professionally followed my instructions and then turned to me for more. "Now tell them that there are many, many universities and language schools in Hefei that pay 100 Yuan per hour. I have never taught for less than 200 Yuan per hour – and that's the truth! Tell them that," I insisted. "I'll try, but your message is very direct and they may not understand and may even be offended." Jane cautioned.

"Just tell them exactly what I have said. Please do it!" I said this in very matter of fact tone. She obediently did as she was instructed and the two guests responded as anticipated with looks of discouragement and helplessness on their faces. They spoke something and Jane said they would like to do that, but they would have to discuss it and maybe communicate with the foundation that helped to support them. They promised me that they would try to find a way to meet my requirements. It seemed that they were willing to do anything to secure my help.

That's exactly what I wanted to see. I was satisfied and said, "Look, I'll make you a deal you can't refuse. I'll agree to teach you to speak English for one week at no charge if you will do everything I tell you to do. I mean everything! If you don't like my rules then you can find yourself another teacher." Jane translated and the two men happily agreed. Then after a short pause, Jane asked what the conditions were.

"All right, the first thing is that in order to learn to speak English you need to speak every day! I mean every day! So the first rule is that we will have a class for at least an hour every day at 1:00 p.m. They will have to find a classroom and tell us where it is. If they would rather take a rest after lunch, then they must not want to learn to speak English very badly. Tell them that," I insisted.

Without hesitation they enthusiastically agreed. Passing up their customary rest time after lunch showed me a very high level of commitment on their part.

"Next, they must be willing to participate and speak, and there will be homework every day they will need to do. If they don't do it, I'm out of here. They will need to make everyone a copy of this booklet called *10 Secrets to Accelerated English Fluency* and the *Instant English* materials. That will be the only textbook we will use. Once we become familiar with it, we will get rid of it. Make that clear to them." She did and again they nodded in agreement.

"Finally, I want them to make me a picture name card for every student the size of a business card. Next to their picture, I want them to clearly write their USTC student number, name in pin yin and their English name if they have one. Then at the bottom, I want their e-mail address and a telephone number if they have it so I can communicate with them if I need to. When they have all this, I'll begin teaching. As soon as they bring it to me, we can begin the class the next day," I concluded, and sat back in my chair to relax.

After they had gone, Mary-Jo asked me, "What did you get yourself into this time?"

"I don't know, it's only an experiment for a week. Maybe they won't show and nothing will happen. If they do come through, it could be very exciting," I said as I shrugged my shoulders and tipped my head. I saw it as an opportunity to test the *10 Secrets* concept on a group in a real teaching situation.

Early the next afternoon, Jane brought over all the printed materials and name cards. "Wow, they must be serious and really want to learn to speak English," I laughed. Jane laughed too and agreed that they really were very grateful for the opportunity. "OK, let's give them their money's worth. I'll see you in class tomorrow at 1 o'clock. Thanks." We both thanked each other and said good-bye as Jane turned to go downstairs and return to her work on campus.

The First Day of Class

At the beginning of the first class, there was a formal introduction. I then rehearsed a detailed review of the interview with Philip and Cari that had resulted in the class being held. I learned that a few of the Tibetan students had taken some classes and had some training in English, but not too much. Some had just begun their studies of the language in classes that were being offered at USTC.

I wanted everyone to be committed so I gave them all the same challenge and threatened not to return the next day if they did not follow my instructions carefully. With Jane's help in translation, I then explained to these quiet and attentive Tibetan students that in almost all of my lectures and conversations with Chinese people, someone always asked the same question, "What is the secret to improving my spoken English?"

"Today, I'm going to give you ten secrets to improving and even accelerating your English speaking ability. They will help you understand some of the reasons for the difficulties you are having and they will also give you the principles and practices in overcoming these difficulties."

Everyone seemed so excited and very fortunate to be receiving the magic that would make them instant English speakers and to help them speak fluently without fear and to speak English well.

Background

I explained and Jane translated, "Chinese people study English for many years. They learn grammar and have a very good vocabulary, but they continue to have difficulty in speaking. There are several key obstacles that cause this phenomenon which can quickly and easily be overcome. One of the biggest obstacles is fear! There is also the obstacle of not wanting to say the wrong thing or to say something incorrectly. Another obstacle is the need and habit to mentally translate from Chinese to English and then to convert these thoughts into spoken words and sentences. Many of these difficulties are caused by the way Chinese people study and learn the English Language."

Learning Language

I insisted that if they wanted to learn to speak English that they must, "Learn to speak as a child learns to speak. Learning to understand and speak a language is one of the first skills a child develops. Small children are capable of learning many languages at the same time. They listen for a time and then they try to repeat. Usually, their learning environment is very friendly and encouraging. Parents give great praise for the smallest efforts and slightest improvements."

Then I explained, "The child develops positive self-esteem and courage and is excited about learning. Remember, it is a long time before a child knows anything about grammar, spelling or formal sentence structure. Their whole focus is on speaking and communicating."

All the students nodded in agreement. This wasn't hard. This was just good old common sense.

I then raised an important warning to "Avoid criticism and give generous praise. Language teachers should avoid criticism and be very encouraging and generous with praise. If someone is lazy or doesn't like to learn to speak a new language, the best way to motivate them is to praise them for their efforts and never criticize. Criticism or pointing out faults too often causes the student to be apprehensive and they lose self-confidence and develop fear of speaking." I reassured all the students that they did not need to be afraid of making mistakes and that I would not criticize them. I was there to help and encourage them. I was there to teach them. They had no need to be afraid. As Winston Churchill famously said, "The only thing we have to fear is fear itself." This would be one of the keys to their success: No fear!

Like in Christina Li's class where the *Seven Secrets* had first come to me, I explained how "learning to speak any language is a right-brain activity. Other right-brain activities or qualities include physical movement and coordination, art, music, creativity and imagination. The left side of our brain masters the very orderly and structured things like memorization, mathematics, science, logical thinking, and accounting, etc. This was an easy way for everyone to visualize and understand how the mind works in the language learning process.

Jane carefully translated and answered the students questions, everyone understood, I continued, "Young Chinese children learn to speak Chinese using the right side of their brain. Then when they go to school they begin learning Chinese by using their left-brain. Perhaps because the Chinese language requires a lot of memorization of Chinese characters etc., the science of the language is learned or understood in a very left brained manner."

I explained that while they, the Tibetan students, were having difficulty learning to speak English, I was having equal difficulty learning to speak Chinese. My teachers and textbooks insisted on learning so many things before getting around to actually speaking.

"I don't want to offend anyone," I said. There are some great things about China, its culture and its educational system. However there are some drawbacks too. The same applies to the United States and any other country's educational system. No one has a perfect system and no one has perfect students," I had Jane carefully translate. <u>The Chinese language demands and the Chinese educational system promotes left brain development</u>. Because of the very nature of the Chinese educational system's focus on learning information, memorizing, scientific focus and its testing and advancement methods, we find that Chinese students excel in these areas. However, these same students have great difficulty in being able to speak or otherwise verbalize the English language. One of their greatest desires is to speak English fluently, but this is also their biggest fear. They fear that they will make mistakes and not speak correctly or that they will be criticized.

The lights began to go on in their minds. Yes, this explained some of their own frustrations and answered some of their questions as to why speaking English seemed so difficult. Silently, they were asking themselves, "Why hadn't someone thought of this before and why are we doing this to ourselves?" Perhaps it was because teachers and professors over the years had developed a system that could be written into books and measured by taking examinations. The focus had been on the exam score and not on the person's ability to communicate. The feedback had resulted in criticism and fear of failure rather than realizing that trial and error was essential to improvement. Nobody wanted to fail. Therefore, nobody was learning to speak English. Speaking was not a big part of the classroom experience.

I explained that, very often, this is an obstacle or challenge too big for many Chinese people to overcome. They continue to diligently study the science of the language and develop a large vocabulary and understanding of grammar rules etc., but they continue to neglect their speaking skills.

The "Mute" Language

Before I could teach them anything, I thought it was important for all the students to understand that, most diligent students of the English language are often frustrated because they just can't seem to access their knowledge and get it out of their mouths. For this reason, many of them call it a 'mute' language. They understand it and can read and write it, but they cannot speak it! This seemed to get a real strong response from everyone because they could relate so much to what I was saying. They were doing everything they could, but sometimes it just didn't seem to work for them.

Purpose

I continued, "The purpose of the *10 Secrets to Speaking English* is to provide key principles, activities and methods of measurement that everyone can use to improve their speaking ability. The goal of these secrets is to help people enjoy learning and to communicate fluently in English. Speakers can now have the tools and skills along with a friendly environment where they can overcome their fears, and enjoy and measure their progress through personal effort and competition with others."

Guarantee

As I spoke, Jane continued to translate. Through her, I promised them, "If you use the *10 Secrets* correctly and follow them diligently, you will succeed. I guarantee you that your speaking fluency will not only increase dramatically, but it will accelerate. You do not need a foreigner or native English speaker to improve your spoken English. Yes, that would be a wonderful advantage, but you can dramatically improve on your own by following these guidelines. That's a promise and that's my guarantee! Practice each of the *10 Secrets* and record your progress every day and you will see remarkable results," I challenged.

Recording & Scoring Results

"A great man named Thomas Monson once said something like, 'If you measure your performance, your performance will improve.'"

I let that idea soak in for a few minutes until I was satisfied that everyone both understood and accepted the concept.

Then I continued, "So now I want to give you a simple way to measure your spoken English 'performance'. OK? This simple method will remind you to do each of the activities. It will require you to keep a record of your progress and will show you where you are putting the most effort and where you need to improve. So, at the end of each day simply give yourself an honest and objective evaluation of how you did during that day. Give yourself a number score from 0 to 10 in each activity area."

"Remember, this is not rocket science. It's really very simple, so keep it simple!" I pleaded. I wrote on the blackboard and slowly repeated each value, "The numbers represent the following rating: 0 = no effort or failure to perform; 1 = very poor effort; 2 = little effort; 3 = not so good effort; 4 = below average; 5 = average effort; 6 = above average effort; 7 = very good effort; 8 = a lot of effort; 9 = excellent effort; 10 = perfect or maximum score available."

"Does everyone understand?" I asked. There were some questions and answers and then I said, "Add the total score for each day and then the total score for the whole week or month. You can follow your progress on the chart by plotting your cumulative average of your weekly scores. Just add up all the weekly scores and divide by the total number of weeks. That will give you your cumulative score. You may also like to prepare your own spreadsheet on your computer. You can quickly and easily calculate and plot your scores. If you are not sure how to do it, you can ask a friend who is a computer expert." (See the charts at the back of the book.)

YES! Your English Secrets!

I stepped into the middle of the class and looked around. "Are you ready!" I shouted. The loud statement seemed to shock the students and they didn't know quite how to respond. I smiled broadly and more quietly asked, "Are you ready? Are you ready now to learn the *10 Secrets*?" Now they understood and a few clapped while everyone answered, "Yes".

I went back to the front of the class and opened my arms very wide as to include everyone. "Alright, I'll share them with you. But, you must know that from this day forward, your life will never be the same. Then I turned and began to write the following list of the *10 Secrets* on the blackboard. I repeated them again and Jane again translated, "The following are your *10 Secrets* to improving your English speaking ability. After you read these secrets and use them, your life will never be the same! Good luck and enjoy the journey".

The students watched as I slowly and deliberately wrote the title of each secret by its number.

1. Self-Esteem/Self-Talk
2. Teach Others

3. Sing Songs
4. Talk to the TV & Radio
5. Read Aloud & Read A Lot
6. Call Others on the Telephone
7. Group Participation
8. Interpret For Others
9. Memorize New Words & Phrases
10. Read, Write and Memorize Poetry

The class sat quietly listening to me say each one in English and then turning their head toward Jane as she said the same thing in Chinese. One by one they watched their future unfold before them.

When I was finished, I turned to them and pointed to the list on the board. "So there you are, 10 easy exercises you can do every day, on your own or with your friends. They won't cost you a penny, only some time and consistent effort and dedication. If you measure your progress each day, each week and each month you will visually see your progress improve and even accelerate. Let me remind you again, you are only competing with yourself, so be honest in your evaluation and scoring".

I had the class repeat each one and challenged them to memorize the list as part of their homework. After a quick review of the Instant English material, the class was dismissed with an assignment to try to do each of the 10 Secrets that night for homework after they had read the materials. There was a loud and enthusiastic applause as I waved good-bye through the doorway.

Your Dreams Can Come True

After a few days of euphoria, good participation and dramatic progress on the part of each student, I thought it would be a good time to include some motivation along with the speaking exercises. Towards the end of one of the classes, I began my little speech by saying, "Your dream to speak English fluently can and will come true. Just remember that wherever you are in your progress, your English is very good. Remind yourself that you are making excellent progress."

"Is there room for improvement? Of course there is room for improvement. You can even improve on your spoken Chinese. Did you ever stop to realize that even your spoken Chinese is not perfect?" Everyone laughed. "That's OK. My spoken English is not perfect and I'm a native English speaker. I too am always trying to improve my spoken English. Perhaps you may even speak better English than I do, but maybe you don't believe it. Because you don't believe it, you don't have the confidence and you don't speak. That's a pity."

With all my energy and persuasion I pleaded, "Believe me, your English is good and it's getting better. As you progress, your self-esteem will improve and your confidence will grow. Soon, your ability to speak and to express yourself will surprise you. There will even come a time when you will begin to dream in English."

After Jane translated that statement, everyone laughed and began speaking to one another in Tibetan.

"Yes, dream in English. It's better than dreaming in color. When you dream in English you will know that you are making great progress in your spoken English. You will know that your dream to speak good English is actually coming true."

I told them that class was over for that day, but they were able to stay and just talk if they did it in English. I put my water bottle, the name cards and other papers in my briefcase and turned toward the door. Halfway there I paused and said, "Good luck to you! May all your dreams come true and may you live happily today and for ever after. I love you all!"

Review: Recording & Scoring Your Results

Jane stayed behind to help a few students who did not completely understand the method of recording or scoring. She explained again that, "These simple methods will:

1. Remind you to do the activity;
2. Require you to keep a record of your progress; and
3. Show you where you are putting the most effort and where you need to improve.

At the end of each day or week simply give an honest and objective evaluation of how you did during that day or week." She carefully reviewed the information and concluded the tutoring session by showing how to score on the board.

Scoring Review

At the end of <u>each day</u> and <u>each week</u>, simply give yourself an honest evaluation of how you did during that day. Give yourself a number score from 0 to 10 in each activity area. The numbers represent the following rating:

0 = no effort or failure to perform
1 = very poor effort
2 = little effort
3 = not-so-good effort
4 = below average effort
5 = average effort
6 = above average effort
7 = very good effort
8 = a lot of effort
9 = excellent effort
10 = perfect or maximum score available

Daily Total Score = the total of the daily scores for each area.

Weekly Total Score = the total of all the scores for each item.

Average = the overall total cumulative score divided by the number of days or weeks recorded.

Chapter 1

Confidence & Self Talk

"Somehow I can't believe that there are any heights that can't be scaled by a man who knows the secrets of making dreams come true. This special secret, it seems to me, can be summarized in four C s. They are curiosity, confidence, courage, and constancy, and the greatest of all is confidence. When you believe in a thing, believe in it all the way, implicitly and unquestionably."
  - Walt Disney

But Professor Dale, it's hard!

Perhaps it was just my personality that seemed to enable those who needed to confess their fears and weaknesses or feelings of inadequacies. On the other hand, maybe it was just those Chinese who felt overwhelmed by the seemingly impossible task of having to succeed in the Chinese educational system or professional marketplace. At any rate, there were at least quite a few who confided their self-doubts and fears to me, their professor and friend.

I was sympathetic to their concerns and fear because I had seen firsthand what critical teachers can do to a student's self-esteem. Instead of encouraging them, teachers often unknowingly create more fear by criticizing. Criticism will come so we need to deal with it. Abraham Lincoln said, "If I care to listen to every criticism, let alone act on them, then this shop may as well be closed for all other businesses. I have learned to do my best, and if the end result is good then I do not care for any criticism, but if the end result is not good, then even the praise of ten angels would not make the difference."

I would try to encourage the students to have faith in themselves and not get discouraged or give up. However; at some point, they would inevitably begin to evangelize and try to convince me how difficult things were and how impossible their goals seemed. When they did this, I usually would try to encourage them and try to get them to focus on the positive things not the negative things. I would tell them about Helen Keller who became famous and very productive after struggling for years as a blind and deaf child, unable to communicate with anyone.

When some went on and on about their fear of failure, I would then tell them that failure was a necessary part of life. Without failure we could not learn. "Failure is the mother of success." "The roses of success rise from the ashes of defeat," and so on. Many times I reminded them of Thomas Edison who failed over 900 times before he discovered how to successfully make a light bulb. When someone asked him if he wasn't tired of failure, he enthusiastically responded, "Why no! I've just discovered over 900 ways not to make the light bulb." He kept going and changed the world!

I soon learned that Chinese people are indeed very much like other people. They shared the same concerns and had the same hopes and dreams that I had. There were some things I knew I could share with them that would help them succeed. I could help them understand the power of a positive attitude and the importance of correct thinking.

YES! Your English Secret to Confidence and Positive Self-Esteem

Each day, the class members met a half hour or an hour early to practice. "Hey, that's a great song! I could hear you singing it all the way down the hall. Keep up the good work." All the Tibetan students were soon ready and waiting to focus on the first of the 10 Secrets as their lesson for the day. "Today is a very nice day," I began. "Yes, today is a very nice day," the class answered.

"As you know, today we are going to focus on secret number one of the *10 Secrets*. This morning I was trying to think of a way to remember each secret. I decided that the word 'yes' can help us to remember 'Your English secret'. What do you think?" I asked. The class thought it was novel idea. "OK, the following is the first of your ten English secrets to improving your speaking ability. Can someone tell me what it is?" "Confidence, Self-Esteem and Postive Self Talk," was the answer from several students.

"Exactly! The most important aspect of speaking is having good self-esteem. Self-esteem is how you feel about yourself. It includes how you think and what you say to yourself or 'self talk'. What you feel determines what you think and what you think determines what you say and how you say it. If you feel good about yourself, you will say good things and speak well. If you feel bad things about yourself, you will think negative thoughts. You will not have self-confidence. Instead you will have fear and you will not speak."

Jane carefully translated to insure that everyone understood the details of what I was saying. It was still too early for them to understand many of the words written in the 10 Secrets. Their assignment was to look up all the words in the dictionary that they did not know. They knew the definitions, but not the meaning to some words or the context in which they used them in a sentence. I knew this from my business classes so I was careful to help everyone with this.

"You know, it's interesting that when most Chinese people are asked how their English is or if they are told their English is very good, they immediately respond by saying, 'Oh, my English is very poor. I have no chance to practice.' Don't say this to yourself and do not say it to others. If you say it often enough, you will begin to believe it and soon you will be paralyzed and unable to speak. You will begin to forget what you know because your right brain cannot speak or use the knowledge you have stored in your left-brain."

I tried to persuade them to look at things differently and change their thinking and behavior. "In learning to speak English, you must put the Chinese custom of modesty or humility aside. When someone compliments you, just say, 'Thank you'. If someone asks how your English is or criticizes you, respond in a positive manner by saying something like, 'I love to speak English.' or 'My English is improving.' or 'I am working very hard to improve my English.' I promised them that these positive statements would reinforce positive thoughts and good feelings.

I tried to dramatically emphasize that, "With increased confidence, you will overcome fear and speak more freely. Your mind is the most fantastic computer in the universe. Don't unplug it or give it deadly viruses by thinking or saying negative things to yourself or others. Remember that your mental computer has a built-in speaker, so use it. Your positive or negative attitude is the on-off switch and your self-esteem is the volume control. Turn it on and turn up the volume and speak, speak, speak!"

I finished the class by having each student commit to doing it - thinking positively and speaking positive things 'about' themselves and 'to' themselves. This new idea was exciting to the class. It seemed to open up so many possibilities in their minds. "Don't get discouraged when things get tough," I said encouragingly. Here is a poem I wrote some time ago called 'Always Say I Can'":

Life brings a daily challenge each one of us must meet.
How we meet that challenge brings success or mere defeat.
It doesn't really matter if the task is great or small.
Your attitude determines if you rise or if you fall.
So think of possibilities and always say "I can."
And life's challenges will find a happy succeeding man.

Then I gave each a small handout including this poem and some other quotes and ideas. This homework should be fun! I left and the students began to read and discuss the following material:

Secrets to Better Thinking and Better Attitudes or B-Attitudes

"No pessimist ever discovered the secrets of the stars, or sailed to an unchartered land, or opened a new haven to the human spirit."
  - Helen Keller

"Your mind is a 'thought factory.' It's a busy factory, producing countless thoughts in one day. Production in your thought factory is under the charge of two foremen, one of whom we will call Mr. Triumph and the other Mr. Defeat. Mr. Triumph is in charge of manufacturing positive thoughts. He specializes in producing reasons why you can, why you're qualified, why you will. The other foreman, Mr. Defeat, produces negative, depreciating thoughts. He is your expert in developing reasons why you can't, why you're weak, why you're inadequate. His specialty is the 'why-you-will-fail' chain of thoughts. Both Mr. Triumph and Mr. Defeat are intensely obedient. They snap to attention immediately. All you need do to signal either foreman is to give the slightest mental beck-and-call. If the signal is positive, Mr. Triumph will step

forward and go to work. Likewise, a negative signal brings Mr. Defeat forward."
   - David J. Schwartz, *The Magic of Thinking Big* p. 18.

". . . the world's most deadly disease – 'Hardening of the Attitudes'. Our success and happiness is largely determined by how we feel about ourselves and others and the world around us. How we feel is determined by how we think and reason. In his book As A Man Thinketh, *James Allen states, 'Your attitude is more important than your mental capacity.' It's your attitude that determines your altitude, not how big or smart or how beautiful you are or whether you have lots of money or political influence. Knowing this we can determine our own destiny."*
   - *See You At The Top*, Zig Ziglar

Wilford Gardner said, "We must be a thermostat instead of a thermometer." We should regulate and direct our lives and not just react to what is happening.

Paul H. Dunn said, "There are three kinds of people: 1) Those few who make things happen, 2) the many who just watch things happen and 3) a whole lot of people who wonder what happened! We can and should be like the few who make things happen."

A Roman General once said, "If a thing is possible it is done. If a thing is impossible, it will be done."

The poet McLandburgh Wilson wrote, "Twix optimist and pessimist, The difference is droll, the optimist sees the doughnut; The pessimist, the hole. Two men looked out through the self-same bars, one saw mud, and the other saw stars."

The philosopher Ralph Waldo Emerson wrote, "Many people see things as they are and ask why; others see things as they can be and ask why not?"

Cervantes, the great winter and author of *Don Quixote*, wrote, "Man should see the world, not as it is, but as it should be."

I strongly believe that it is so important that we always have a positive attitude. It depends on our thinking. With a positive attitude our world will be better and more beautiful and we will succeed in life. We will learn that life is the process of finding out who we really are and achieving whatever we can conceive. To help me express this idea better, I wrote the following poem many years ago. I titled it "Common Thought":

It's a common thing to think a thought,
  of things we are and things we're not.
In deep despair one starts to sink,
  if we entertain such thoughts to think.
But if we change the way we think,
  we'll always rise and never sink.
We'll create our world and love a lot,
  for such is born in common thought.

Business Attitudes or B-Attitudes

In any business, positive attitude is important. In the textbook *Management Communication: Principles and Practice* by Michel E. Hattersley and Lind McJannet, they give a list of ethical imperatives (or business commandments:):

1. Avoid harming other.
2. Respect the rights of others.
3. Do not lie or cheat.
4. Keep promises and contracts.
5. Obey the law.
6. Prevent harm to others.
7. Help those in need.
8. Be fair.
9. Reinforce these imperatives in others.

I add

10. You are your most important customer, so be positive.

I call these "business attitudes" or the "B-Attitudes". Common sense dictates that the benefactors of those practicing these B-attitudes do not do things that enable others to take advantage of them or to be lazy. The idea is to help others to help themselves. If they do then the helper will prosper from their efforts.

Another B-Attitude would be the "banquet attitude" where it would be ideal if our nations, companies and business people could do business in a spirit of service and mutual benefit. Following a delicious banquet and stimulating discussion about how the restaurant business Jinmanlou Chain Enterprise could expand their market, I wrote the General Manager, Xu Hua, and said, "The dining table is often the best place for sharing ideas and for developing plans and meaningful relationships. Like great recipes for delicious and nourishing dishes, ideas and relationships are mixed in the environment of hospitality, seasoned with friendship, warmed with trust and then shared generously for the benefit of all who partake." Many relationships are developed and business deals made around the dining table. Wouldn't it be wonderful if the same spirit of hospitality, enjoyment and concern for our guest's satisfaction could carry over into all aspects of our lives including our negotiations and permeate our contracts, production and conflict resolutions?"

Booker T. Washington wrote in his book *Up From* Slavery, "I think I began learning that those who are happiest are those who do the most for others. No man who continues to add something to the material, intellectual and moral well being of the place in which he lives is long left without proper reward. This is a great human law that cannot be permanently nullified."

10 Secrets to Improved People Skills

In the book *How To Win Friends and Influence People*, the author summarized the basic techniques in how to successfully work with people, help them to like you, influence their thinking, help them change, and have a happier home life. We all would be wise to take inventory on how we measure up to these 10 suggestions to always try to improve:

1. Give honest praise continually, never criticize or argue.
2. See things from the other person's point of view.
3. Be interested in others and do things for them.
4. Call people by name - make them feel important.
5. Listen intently and let the other person do the talking.
6. Talk to people about their interests.
7. Make the other person feel important.
8. Admit you're wrong quickly and emphatically.
9. Let the other feel it was his idea.
10. Appeal to the nobler motives and be courteous and smile.

Ancient Chinese Proverb

He who <u>knows not</u> and <u>knows not</u> that he knows not,
he is a fool. Shun *him.*
He who <u>knows not</u> and <u>knows</u> that he knows not,
he is simple. Teach *him.*
He who <u>knows</u> and <u>knows not</u> that he knows,
he is asleep. Wake *him.*
He who <u>knows</u> and <u>knows</u> that he knows,
he is wise. Follow *him.*

My friend Lu Wei says it this way, "Avoid unconscious incompetence, teach the conscious incompetent, wake up the unconscious competent and follow the consciously competent."

Chapter 2

Teach Others

Teachers Pay

To: Dale - Dear Dale, Nice to seeing you and your family! Today, when you leave the classroom, some boy of our class shouted, "Wow! Dale, you are a superior, you are a great man. Yes, you are. We all love you. I like to see film. In most of film, the businessman always fat, unkind and greedy. but you are not. You are like a scholar and artist, humor and versatile. We are all think that you are a really gentleman. I don't known how to make you to understand our thought.. No matter you whether continued teach us, we all feel grateful of you for your help! Thank you again!"

Speak Everyday

Over and over again, I emphasized the importance of speaking English everyday, having class every day and using the 10 Secrets every day. I would have all the students repeat after me, "I will speak English every day!" "I will attend class every day." And, "I will use the 10 Secrets every day." I promised them that if they did this for at least 21 days then they would develop strong and good speaking habits. However, even with this emphasis on speaking every day, I advised them to rest one day each week so they would not get tired, bored or burned out. "Work hard for six days and then rest on the seventh," I would advise them. I can't explain it to you, but you will progress faster if you follow that formula."

Everyone was practicing and warming up with the familiar speaking drills at the beginning of class. It had been going on for about fifteen minutes when I stopped in mid-sentence and said, "Oh, I almost forgot. Next week is the May holiday and I will be traveling to Guilin and Yangshuo with my family." I asked if anyone else had plans to travel during the holiday. Everyone planned to stay on campus and promised to continue holding classes. "OK, who would like to be our teacher for those days. How about we rotate the assignment each day it so several of you get a chance to teach the class?"

Everyone sat silent until Irene slowly raised her hand to volunteer. Then another and another volunteered until all the days were covered. "Very good," I commended. "You will progress faster than the others because you will be teaching. You see what I do. Just try to do the same things to get everyone speaking in class. Remember that participation is the key and getting everyone involved and speaking is the best method of teaching in this class."

I reviewed the pattern of how to conduct the class and what exercises to go over and then promised the volunteer teachers that they would be happy they had volunteered to teach.

Then I began the exercise with everyone repeating after me, "I am a teacher. You are a teacher. He is a teacher. She is a teacher. We are teachers. They are teachers. I am a good teacher. You are a good teacher. He is a good teacher. We are very good teachers. They are very good teachers. I like to teach. You like to teach. She likes to teach. We like to teach very much. They like to teach very much" and so on. Everyone felt a lot more confident after repeating several times the idea behind the secret being discussed that day. Teach others. After one of the classes, I received my biggest pay check in the e-mail message at the beginning of this chapter.

Good Teachers Are the Best Students

Then I gave them a little lecture to give them some rationale behind the Secret #2 Teaching Others. "It is a known fact," I said, "that the teacher learns more than the student. People receive more when they give. When you only receives, you become dependent, then crippled, and become unable to give. A person can even die."

I whirled around to look for a piece of chalk big enough to draw a picture to help explain my next thoughts. While I erased what was on the blackboard, I continued talking, "First of all, when you teach someone else to speak English you forget yourself and concentrate on helping someone else. This is a key process in learning. You actually get more when you give more. You get better at speaking when you give others instructions and encouragement."

I asked if everyone understood. They did. Then I asked if anyone agreed with me or disagreed. No one offered a response, but by the look on their faces and the nodding of their heads, I could tell that they were with me and agreed. Almost all of them had been teachers for a few years and knew the value of preparing and teaching and how they benefited.

I went on, "Secondly, when you teach you are forced to use all the skills of speaking well. You must remember that which you have stored in your left-brain, move it to the right side, translate it from Chinese into English and then you have to verbalize it. You must speak it to teach it. You hear yourself speak and can recognize your own needs and correct yourself while you teach, correct and encourage your student(s). It's a great method and a self-motivating process." I used my hands and body language to point and motion to my heart for feeling, both sides of my head to emphasize the right and left-brain connection and to my mouth giving the gesture of words flowing from it.

Then I drew a map on the blackboard with a line representing a river flowing from the top into a small circle and then another line flowing into a larger circle. Continuing with great emphasis, I said, "For thousands of years, this method has been a powerful secret to learning. To compare the difference in just receiving and taking and learning and giving, let me tell you about two famous seas, the Sea of Galilee and the Dead Sea found in the country of Israel. The Sea of Galilee is much smaller and lies to the north. It receives water in and also generously gives water out through the Jordan River that flows south into the Dead Sea. The Sea of Galilee is full of fish and plant life and provides food and life for many. On the other hand, the Dead Sea only takes and gives nothing back in return except salt. No fish or plant life can live there. If only the Dead Sea could give water out, it could become alive again. That's how we are as teachers."

Everyone seemed very pleased with the explanation and there was a new spirit of confidence and energy in the room. They recognized that they were students of English who were trying to learn to speak this new language. However, instead of just learning how to speak they were learning "how to learn" to speak and "how to teach" others how to speak. In just a few weeks and months they would have to teach others these 10 Secrets and teach others how to speak and how to become teachers too. I encouraged them with, "Remember, teach others and your rate of progress will surprisingly improve."

Instant English For Beginners

Ben enthusiastically raised his hand to make a comment. "Yes Ben," I invited. "I speak English very good! I am a good teacher!" said Ben with confidence and with a big grin on his happy face. Then, slowly his expression changed to one of concern, and he slowly continued in a very serious tone, "But what do I teach?"

"That's a very good question Ben." Then looking at the rest of the class, I instructed the class, "Do as you have seen me do. Teach what I have taught you and in the same way. You can use your own personality and any other methods that help you. But if you don't know what to do, just ask yourself what I would do and then do it. Teach how I have taught you and make it fun and enjoyable for everyone. I believe that speaking a new language is not as hard as it's made out to be. You don't need to study books and learn how to write before you can speak. As a matter of fact, I believe that speaking English is something that everyone can do and do it almost immediately."

I explained that by learning some simple concepts and words and how to use them, a person can immediately begin to speak sentences in English and be very well understood. "A friend's young son recently came to China from Pakistan. Even though my friend had been taking Chinese classes for many months, his son quickly began to teach him the meaning of words and how to speak sentences. Almost immediately he surpassed his father in his ability to communicate. The difference was that my friend was learning Chinese the traditional way and his son was learning how to speak. Each day his son would learn from his classmates the meaning of words and speak in sentences. The father was learning the language the 'traditional way' and the son was learning to speak in the 'instant' way.

I reminded them that their minds were magnificent and were better than any computer and would do great things if they just had confidence in it. In the most challenging tone I could use, I said, "Let me also say that I believe that any

Chinese person can learn to speak English regardless of age or education. Many people believe it is much easier for children to learn a new language than adults. It's not the age that makes the difference; it's how you learn. You must learn to speak as a child learns to speak. Actually, the more education and training in the 'science of the English language' the more difficulty you may have in speaking. It isn't because your education is bad. It's because you are learning everything else about the language except how to speak. A child learns how to speak, but doesn't know much else."

"If this is true, that means that your parents or your favorite uncle or friend, who perhaps is afraid to learn English, can learn to speak and enjoy it," I said. "They don't have to learn all the many details and rules. They just need to learn some basic skills for instant English for beginners and they can soon be communicating in Basic English. It's really not as difficult as it seems," I concluded in a matter of fact tone. "I think that this is exciting news. Now it would be much easier if I could explain these things in person to the beginner. But since I'm not there, you will have to do it for me. By explaining the information you learn using this secret, you can help teach the beginner to immediately begin to speak English."

Again the class followed the exercise, "Speaking is easy. Speaking is natural. Speaking English is easy. English is not difficult. Speaking is not difficult." I asked each class member to answer the questions, "Is speaking English easy? Is speaking English difficult? And, are you a good speaker?" Each student would reply, "Yes, speaking English is easy. No, speaking English is not difficult. And, "Yes, I am a good English speaker."

Then I told the class about a friend who had shared an idea with him that was helping old people to speak sentences in a new language only after a few hours of training and practice. These older people overcame their fears and gained confidence, once they realized that they could make many simple sentences out of a few verbs. They also felt great relief once they realized that they didn't need to know a lot of the "science of the language" in order to speak.

Science of the English Language

I wrote on the blackboard the key words that I was trying to explain, "The science of the English language includes so many things like learning the alphabet, correct spelling, grammar rules, memorizing lots of words and phrases, learning to read and write. Learning to speak begins with listening and watching the body language. These two things come naturally with speaking. We must frequently remind beginners that they should only be interested in speaking. Don't trouble yourselves with all the other many details, rules and skills. You can learn those things later."

Focus on Speaking

Almost instinctively, everyone wrote down what I was saying as if this were an important part of helping him or her learn to speak. I interrupted them and ordered them to put down their pens. I explained that if they had to write everything down in order to study so they could speak then they would be working against themselves. Almost pleading, I said, "Keep focused on speaking. You may be just beginning to learn English or you may have studied for many years. Regardless of your past experience or ability, this chapter will focus only on speaking simple English sentences. You will not be burdened by trying to learn the science of the English language. The purpose of this class and these secrets is to help you to speak simple English in a very short time and to communicate effectively. If that is your interest then you are in the right place. If not, you are in the wrong place! So don't worry about writing or taking notes. I'll give you what you need. Just focus on speaking." I then shared the following basics of simple language and how they could quickly learn for themselves and learn how to teach others:

Who Does What? Almost every sentence is in the form of "who does what".

WHO? = (subject)

The following examples are those "who", that are the subject of almost all simple sentences. You can easily remember them by using the fingers on your hand. You can use your hand to remember whom you are speaking to or talking about. A friend once suggested this method to me. Try it as follows:

1. Your thumb points to you and represents the 1st person (I, me, my, mine).
2. Your first finger or index finger represents the 2nd person (you, your, yours).
3. The middle finger represents the 3rd person singular (he, she, it, this, that, his, hers, its, him, her).
4. The fourth finger or ring finger represents the plural 1st person (we, us, our, ours).
5. The fifth or little finger represents the 3rd person plural (they, them, these, those, their, theirs, its).

The open hand represents "all" and the closed hand or a fist represents "none" or "no one ". Altogether, you have 32 people to speak to or talk about.

1. I, me, my, mine
2. You, your, yours
3. He, she, it, this, that, his, hers, its, him, her
4. We, us, our, ours

5. They, them, these, those, their, theirs, its
6. All, everyone, none, no one

First, learn them in Chinese (wo, ni, ta, women, nimen, tamen) on your fingers and then learn them in English. You will use your fingers to help you begin simple sentences using the following 10 plus 3 verbs and other verbs as you progress:

10 + 3 Basic Verbs (Infinitive = to __)

Using the right "who" along with a combination of the following 10 + 3 verbs, you will be able to say hundreds of simple sentences. First learn the meaning of the verbs in Chinese.

DOES! = (action – verb)

1. To be
2. To understand
3. To do
4. To go
5. To come
6. To speak
7. To be able to (can)
8. To want
9. To need
10. To have
11. To give
12. To like
13. To love

WHAT? = (object)

Infinitive verb =

Noun =

This, that, these, those =

Make Simple Sentences

When you have mastered the people on your fingers and know the meaning of the verbs you are ready to begin to speak simple sentences. You don't need to write them down or to see anything. All you have to do is think them in your mind and say what you think.

At this point it is important that you don't get into the habit of having to have a book, a blackboard or notepad to read the sentences. Most Chinese people can read English, but speaking it is another matter. You must think it and speak it.

So now formulate a sentence in your mind in Chinese. When you are ready with the idea you want to communicate then use your hand and fingers to say it in English. Using the same words, you can make many different sentences with different meanings just by changing the person. For Example:

The verb to speak:
I speak English.
We speak English.
You speak English very well.

The verb to like:
I like English.
We like English.
They like English very much.

By changing the person (I, you, he, she, we, they etc.) you can speak many different sentences using the same verb. By adding another verb (the infinitive to ____) you can make more complex sentences with new meanings.

Combine the 2 verbs (to like & to speak):

I like to speak English

We like to speak English.

They like to speak English very much.

23 Auxiliary Verbs - Memorize and practice the 23 helping or auxiliary verbs so you can use the correct tense in forming almost all sentences.

Am, is, are, was, were, be, being, been, have, has, had, do, does, did, shall, will should, would, may, might, must, can & could.

It is important that you can say what you want. So you must make a list of the words and verbs that you want to use to verbally express yourself. Make this list and then combine it with those presented below to make a complete list to use in our daily speaking.

Useful Words (= means to fill in with the word in your language)

Please =
Thank you =
Friend =
Name =
Man =
Woman =
Boy =
Girl =
Husband =
Wife =
Son =
Daughter =
Father =
Mother =
Brother =
Sister =

Grandfather =
Grandmother =
Baby =
Child =
Uncle =
Aunt =
Nephew =
Niece =
Cousin =
Teacher =
Engineer =
Doctor =
Lawyer =
Businessman =
Partner =
Boss =
Employee =
North =
South =
East =
West =
Up =
Down =
Left =
Right =
Front =
Back =
Above =
Below=

Useful Phrases

I am happy.
He is happy.
She is happy.

It is good.
We are happy.
They are happy.
His was very good.
They were very good.
You be good!
They are being good.
He was very good.
It has been good.
You have been good.
Ours has been easy.
We do very well.
Yours does very well.
Theirs does very well.
I shall speak every day.
I will speak every day.
I should speak more often.
You would like it.
You may speak.
It might work.
It must work.
It can work.
It could work.
It was theirs.
Do it for them.
Those are mine.
They like me.
They like me very much.
You speak English very well.
I like you very much.
I am an English teacher.
I teach people how to speak English.
I teach spoken English.
I like teaching English very much.

Special Verb Uses

Please note that the 3rd person singular will almost always have a <u>different form of the verb</u> so learn these and practice them well. Good luck!

To be =

I am happy.
We are happy.
You are happy.
He/she/it <u>is</u> happy.
They are happy.

I was happy.
We were happy.
You were happy.
He/she/it <u>was</u> happy.
They were happy.

I will be happy.
We will be happy.
You will be happy.
He/she/it will be happy.
They will be happy.

To understand =

To do =

I do this.
We do this.
You do this.
He/she/it <u>does</u> this.
They do this.

Do not =

I do not do this.
We do not do this.
You do not do this.
He/she/it <u>does</u> not do this.
They do not do this.

To go =

I go to school.
We go to school.
You go to school.
He/she/it <u>goes</u> to school.
They go to school.

To come =

I come home.
We come home.
You come home.
He/she/it <u>comes</u> home.
They come home.

To speak =

I speak English.
We speak English.
You speak English.
He/she/it <u>speaks</u> English.
They speak English.

To be able to (can) =

I can speak English.
We can speak English.
You can speak English.
He/she/it can speak English.
They can speak English.

I <u>am</u> able to speak English.
We are able to speak English.
You are able to speak English.
He/she/it <u>is</u> able to speak English.
They are able to speak English. .

To want =

I want food.
We want food.
You want food.
He/she/it <u>wants</u> food.
They want food.

To need =

I need help.
We need help.
You need help.
He/she/it <u>needs</u> help.
They need help.

To have =

I have classes.
We have classes.
You have classes.
He/she/it <u>has</u> classes.
They have classes.

To give =

I give gifts.
We give gifts.
You give gifts.
He/she/it <u>gives</u> gifts.
They give gifts.

Useful Phrases

Hello! How are you?
My name is _____ .
What is your name?
I am 25 years old.
How old are you?
Where is the school?
When is the class?
What is this?
What is that?
What are these?
What are those?
I don't understand what you said.
Please repeat what you said.
Please speak more slowly.
Thank you for your help.
Why do you say it that way?
How do you say _____?
How can I find _____?

Good Questions

What kind of _____ do you like _____?

food	to eat
sports	to play
movies	to watch
books	to read
clothes	to wear
places	to go/to visit
songs	to sing
games	to play
etc.	etc.

Good Answers

(Remember that part of the answer is in the question.)

I like _____ _____.

        to eat   Chinese food
        to play   football
        to watch   action movies
        to read   good books
        etc.   etc.

Chapter 3

Sing Songs

"The hills are alive with the sound of music..."
- Walt Disney

Music Has Magic

This was a new day and a new secret. Today's class was going to focus on singing songs in English to help develop the Tibetan student's fluency. Little did I know how well these people could sing, but neither did they know how their love for singing would help them to speak English better and faster. When I entered the room, the class exchanged their normal greetings and pleasantries in English.

I then leaned on the podium, looked into their eyes and said, "Today, I want to tell you a story about two very special people and how singing helped them speak better English. Not only has singing helped these two people, but singing songs in English has helped millions of people speak better English and it can help you. Did you know that music has magic in it? Yes it does! And the secret is to use that magic to help you speak English."

The students seemed very pleased and seemed eager to know what secret this simple and very obvious activity held in store. Before telling the class about these two people, I continued with my explanation. "Singing songs has magic that no other exercise can duplicate. When you sing songs over and over again, you automatically memorize the words and phrases."

With my arm raised as if to lead a choir, I began to sing *Happy Birthday*, "Haaaappy Birrrrrthdayyyyy ... Tooo Youuu." For a moment, most of the students wondered what I was doing. But, almost instantly some students began to sing along with me. At first they were cautious, but then their voices became louder until everyone who knew the song was singing along and concluded in applause

Without a pause, and this time with a pen in my hand as a director's baton, I began singing in a loud voice and leading them in singing *Jingle Bells*. Some had never heard the song. But for those who knew it, their eyes lit up and they enthusiastically began to sing along until they finished the chorus, "What fun it is to ride and sing a sleighing song tonight".

With the enthusiasm of the moment still in the air, I said, "See how easy it is?" Then one timid student raised his hand and asked, "What is a jingle?" Then another asked, "What is a sleigh?" I was surprised, but soon realized that while they could sing the song, they didn't know the meaning of many of the words they were saying. So I spent the next ten minutes drawing pictures on the blackboard. I first explained the difference between a sled and a sleigh. Then I drew a picture of a horse pulling an open sleigh. I drew pictures of bells on harnesses and the horse's bobbed tails. I then recommended that they go over the songs they learn word for word so they can better understand the meaning of the songs. With that, I put the chalk down and tried to brush all the white chalk dust off my hands. I held up my two chalk white hands and said, "This looks just like snow!"

Returning to my explanation of the power of music, I continued, "When someone says, 'Let's sing *Jingle Bells* or *Happy Birthday*, immediately you begin to sing the song correctly without even thinking about it. There is no hesitation, no translation, and no confusion. You just sing and enjoy. Also, while singing you are practicing saying words and, at the same time, practicing pronunciation because you verbalize each word more slowly and exactly with the music."

Then almost out of habit I began to recite and the class repeated after me, "I sing songs. You sing songs. He sings songs. She sings songs. We sing songs. They sing songs. I sing very well. You sing very well. He sings very well. We sing very well. They sing very well. I like to sing songs in English. You like to sing songs in English. She likes to sing songs in English. We like to sing songs in English. They like to sing songs in English. Everyone sings songs in English."

She Sings! – She Speaks!

After complimenting them on their pronunciation and participation, I said, "Ok, now let me tell you about these two special people. The first story is about my daughter, when she was a little girl. The other story is about my roommate Toby in college." After a long pause for everyone to understand and get ready to follow, I continued, "When Teresa was a little girl, the only words we could get her to say was Mama and No! She just didn't speak. We weren't too worried until her two younger brothers began to speak more than she did. That's when my wife and I began to wonder if everything was all right with her.

"For her birthday, Teresa's grandmother had sent Teresa a special birthday present. It was a picture book with an audiotape that she could listen to. Each page was a different picture with the words to a children's song. Every night we would sing these songs to our children when we put them down for bed. Everyday Teresa would sit on the sofa and turn the pages in the book while the tape played the songs. She never sang along, only listened.

Then one day a miracle happened. After a family outing, we were returning to our home in Waldorf, Maryland. It was quite a long drive down Route #5. All the children were strapped into their baby seats in the back seat of the car, and one by one they fell asleep. Sam and Jon were sound asleep, but Teresa wanted her music book. Mary-Jo and I were in conversation and talking about whatever we had just been doing when all of a sudden Teresa began to sing aloud the first song of the book. We were shocked and so excited that we didn't dare turn around because we didn't want her to stop. When she finished the first song, she went on to sing the second and then the third and so on until she sang all the songs in the book. When she was done, she laid the book down and snuggled with her baby blanket and turned her head to one side to go to sleep."

The class was mesmerized. I walked over and sat on the first row table and continued. "Can you imagine how excited we were? We hadn't heard her say more than one or two words at a time before this, and all of a sudden she had sung every song in the book, word for word. We were so excited that we couldn't wait any longer. We turned around and complimented her and told her how much we loved her. She seemed embarrassed by the praise and shyly blushed and smiled and just continued to try to go to sleep. I was so excited that I stopped the car and got out and shouted at the top of my lungs to all the fields and trees in the countryside that my little girl could talk and sing!"

I explained that from that day on, Teresa began to also speak and to tell the stories about the songs or to sing them word for word. She didn't know how to read or write. She didn't understand grammar or correct pronunciation. She just spoke and sang. Her pronunciation was actually quite good for a new beginner. Hopefully, this story showed how very important it is for students to understand that listening to the songs and then singing the songs over and over would help them to speak English better.

Toby Stuttered Badly

The next story was about one of my college roommates. My roommate was Toby, a young man with bright red hair and lots of freckles. Toby wasn't very tall, but he had a big heart and was very friendly. He was a good student, had a positive attitude and smiled all the time. The biggest challenge for him in college and perhaps in life was that he stuttered. He had a difficult time getting all the words out to complete his sentences.

I had to have Jane translate several words for the class so they could keep up with the stories. Along with the interpreting, definitions and explanations, I explained that Toby couldn't, "Geeegeeegeee get get the wooo wooo words words out v v v veeerrrrr very gooo goog good." Immediately the Tibetan students understood what Toby's problem was and seemed very sympathetic. I explained that Toby was very open about his problem and spoke about it in a matter of fact way without being ashamed. He had a problem and he dealt with it the best he could. One Sunday afternoon while we were just resting in our dorm room and talking about things, I mentioned that I had noticed him singing in church that morning and not stuttering at all. Toby explained that while he had difficulty speaking, he didn't seem to have the same problem when he sang. He said that his father would encourage him to sing out his message if his stuttering got in the way, especially if it was an emergency. To me, that was very interesting to say the least. Toby explained that many people who stuttered could sing without a problem. Some of them were beautiful singers. Toby said, "Somehow, music has magic in it."

"Well," I explained to the class, "that's what music can do for your ability to speak English. So choose good songs and good music with words you want to remember and be able to say. It is amazing how quickly you can learn to speak English by singing. Listen to the songs and understand the meaning of all the words and then just sing, sing sing!"

I ended the class by discussing how the Chinese language has many tones. In a way the language is sung like a song. In the same way, when you sing songs in English your brain can quickly connect the thoughts and meanings with the sounds. Suddenly, you can speak English! I gave them all some songs they could begin to sing and practice. The homework materials included the following songs:

Happy Birthday

*Happy birthday to you. Happy birthday to you.
Happy birthday dear _____. Happy birthday to you.*

Jingle Bells

*Dashing through the snow, in a one-horse open sleigh
Through the fields we go, laughing all the way.
Bells on bob-tail ring, making spirits bright
What fun it is to ride and sing, a sleighing song tonight.*

*Chorus: Jingle bells, jingle bells, jingle all the way,
Oh what fun it is to ride in a one-horse open sleigh.
Oh, jingle bells, jingle bells, jingle all the way.
Oh what fun it is to ride in a one-horse open sleigh.*

*A day or two ago, I thought I'd take a ride
And soon Miss Fanny Bright, was seated by my side;
The horse was lean and lank, misfortune seemed his lot,
We ran into a drifted bank and there we got upsot.*

*Now the ground is white. Go it while you're young,
Take the girls along and sing this sleighing song.
Just bet a bob-tailed bay, two-forty as his speed,
Hitch him to an open sleigh and crack! You'll take the lead.*

Also, I had prepared different words to music that would be interesting and beautiful to listen to. The class enjoyed learning and singing the following songs to familiar music:

Dreaming In English (Sung to the tune of "I'm Dreaming Of A White Christmas")

I'm dreaming that I speak English.
  Just like the native speakers do
With good long phrases,
  Pronunciation,
  To hear the right words as they flow.

I'm dreaming that I speak English.
  With every syllable I hear.
May your words be happy for you.
  And may all your English dreams come true.

My 10 Secrets (Sung to the tune of "Happy Birthday")

My 10 Secrets for you.
  My 10 Secrets for you.
My 10 Secrets dear students.
  My 10 Secrets for you.

Practice Every Day (Sung to the tune of "Jingle Bells")

Say the words. Say the words.
  Say them just this way.
Oh what fun it is to speak
  And practice every day.

Say the words. Say the words.
  Say them just this way.
Oh what fun it is to speak
  And practice every day.

We Speak English (Sung to the tune of "Oh My Darling, Clementine"

Oh my students. Oh my students.
Oh my students. You are mine.
You're my students, special students.
You're my students and you're mine.

Every day now. Every day now,
Every day now. All the time.
We speak English, such good English,
We speak English all the time.

Oh our teacher. Oh our teacher.
Oh our teacher. You're so fine.
You're our teacher, special teacher.
You're our teacher and you're fine.

Every day now. Every day now,
Every day now. All the time.
You teach English, such good English,
You teach English all the time.

We work so hard. We work so hard.
We work so hard, to speak well.
The words are ours and ours forever.
Oh my English spoken well.

We need teachers. We need students.
Oh we need them all so much!
We are growing, ever growing.
Oh, we've grown so very much.

Every day now. Every day now,
Every day now. All the time.
We speak such good, such good English.
And we speak it all the time.

Dale Christensen

Special classmates. Special classmates.
 Special classmates. That we need.
We are all a very special,
 Very special class indeed.

Chapter 4

Talk to the TV & Radio

"Love is the condition in which the happiness of another person is essential to your own."
- Robert Heinlein

"Love and kindness are never wasted. They always make a difference."
- Anais Nin

"To love means loving the unlovable. To forgive means pardoning the unpardonable. Faith means believing the unbelievable. Hope means hoping when everything seems hopeless."
- Gilbert K. Chesterton

"Love is a force more formidable than any other. It is invisible - it cannot be seen or measured, yet it is powerful enough to transform you in a moment, and offer you more joy than any material possession could."
- Barbara De Angelis

Class Warm Up

"Most language classes begin by using familiar verbs like 'to speak' or 'to go'," I began. "Those are good verbs and we will practice them in this class too. But there are two verbs that I think are very important in any language – 'to like' and 'to love'." They are powerful words and not only have a lot of meaning, but can help us in whatever we do.

I continued, "We use these words in so many ways and with so many meanings that I want us to become very comfortable with them. More important than just speaking however, is using them in our everyday speech with our friends and family. These are words that are positive and help build our confidence and to help build others. These words help us become closer friends and to appreciate one another more. With the feeling that these words help to develop we can overcome differences and bad feelings. We can have delightful experience rather than just another event."

Then, I led the class in the exercise they had become familiar with at the beginning of every class. I led out and the class repeated each statement, "I like myself. I like you. You like me. He likes her. She likes him. We like it. They like us. I love myself. I love you. You love me. He loves her. She loves him. We love it. They love us. We love them." And so on, "I like English . . . I love English . . . I like to speak English . . . I love to teach English . . . I like to sing songs . . . I love to talk to the radio and TV . . . I like to call others on the telephone . . . I love group participation . . . I like to interpret for others . . . I love to memorize new vocabulary words and phrases . . . I love to read, write and memorize poetry . . ." All the ideas and secrets were repeated using the different persons. All the members of the class became very familiar and comfortable using the words "like" and "love". Everyone felt and expressed the meaning of these words.

At this point, I had Jane translate so everyone would understand the power of secret number four. The following is a summary of what I said to the class as they listened intently to every word. Occasionally, I would stop and encourage them to just listen and not worry about writing down what I was saying. I could give them notes to read, but listening and speaking was what they should be focusing on and doing.

Logic or Rational Behind This Secret

There are a growing number of English television channels and radio programs being broadcasted throughout China. There is nothing magic about listening or watching the programs. Oh yes, by watching and or listening your listening skills will improve, but just watching and listening won't help improve your speaking skills very much unless you do a lot of it. I mean a lot! Like my daughter Teresa, listening to the same thing over and over again every day for months.

However, if you are willing to make a little extra effort every day by talking to the TV or radio, your English speaking skills will dramatically improve. If the station isn't clear or you can't be there when your English program is on, then buy yourself some VCDs or DVDs and talk to them. That's every bit as good and it may seem even better. The reason these can be better is that you can listen to them over and over again until you understand everything. You can rewind them or go back and re-ask any question or re-say anything you want. However, beware that you don't rely on this method totally because it isn't totally natural. People don't say the same thing over and over again so you can get it. In most conversations you only have one or two chances to hear and understand and respond. The more closely you practice for this, the better off you are. But, these recordings can be a help to you.

At first, most people would think talking to the radio or television is foolish. They are concerned about what their family or friends might think. They feel very awkward speaking to someone who cannot hear them. They feel even more awkward not knowing what to say. This is all very natural. However, let me suggest that no one, including you, feels embarrassed or out of place watching a football match and yelling and screaming at the top of their lungs at the referee or the opposing team who, by the way, cannot hear you; or watching a quiz show and telling the right answer to the contestant and calling them names if they don't take your suggestions. As if they can hear you give your answer and win the prize.

It's very normal for great actors and speakers to practice their lines by speaking to inanimate objects. If this is the case, then why does it seem so different to speak to the TV or radio? It shouldn't! When you are watching or listening to these programs and someone new comes into the room, they quickly get into the spirit of things and soon they are shouting at the referee or giving the quiz show contestants their own answers. It is very common for you to talk about what is happening in Chinese. Why not talk about it in English. Why not talk about it to the radio or TV broadcaster or to the actors. Remember that it's practice. You are practicing with native speakers and that's a good thing to do.

Once you understand what you are doing and once you explain it to your family and friends, they will completely understand and want to do the same thing so they too can improve their spoken English. When you do it together, you all improve. When it becomes understood and is a culturally acceptable behavior, then it is not only accepted, but it will be encouraged. You know how valuable it is so you will have to be the pioneer to help it to become understood and acceptable.

What Can You Say

Ampree's Tibetan name is Ze Ren Yan Pei. This was his first experience to speak English and he enjoyed it very much. He always spoke with a very loud voice and with a big smile. He always had a very positive attitude which was one reason why he was progressing so well. He also had lots of questions and today was no exception. "I like to watch TV and listen to

English," Ampree said. "But, I don't know what to say to the TV or radio."

"That's a good comment Ampree," I replied. "I guess the right answer is to say what you would normally say if you were talking to them in Chinese or Tibetan. Just join whatever conversation there is and talk about whatever they are talking about. For example, if you are watching the news then ask about whatever they are talking about. In any event, you can tell them to slow down or to repeat their comments. They won't do what you ask, but you can always ask. You can ask them to clarify what they are saying, to further explain or to expand on what they are talking about. Tell them that you agree or disagree with them. Compliment them on their thinking or ideas. Tell them if they speak well. Tell them how they look or how they make you feel. Actually, you can say anything you want to and not offend anyone and not be embarrassed."

Conclusion

On several occasions, I had been invited to appear on local or provincial television and radio shows. Each time I shared the *10 Secrets* with the listening audience. There should be English-speaking television and radio programs and channels in your city. Find them and watch and listen to them, but more importantly, talk to them. This may seem strange and your family or friends may think you're crazy, but it is almost as effective as having a foreigner or native English speaker right in our room all the time.

Listening is a great way to learn, but if you speak back and ask questions, then your mind and speech organs benefit as if the TV or radio were a real person. True, the TV and radio will not answer your questions nor will they pause for your comments. Nevertheless, when you do this, your listening skills will improve and your ability to ask good questions and give good answers will also improve.

Try it, you'll like it. You will need to work at it because we are all conditioned and in the habit of just "listening" to the radio and TV. Listening is good, but speaking is better. It makes all the difference!

Chapter 5

Commitment

"Until one is committed, there is hesitancy, the chance to draw back, always ineffectiveness. Concerning all acts of initiative and creation, there is one elementary truth the ignorance of which kills countless ideas and splendid plans: that the moment one definitely commits oneself, then providence moves too. All sorts of things occur to help one that would never otherwise have occurred. A whole stream of events issues from the decision, raising in one's favor all manner of unforeseen incidents, meetings and material assistance which no man could have dreamed would have come his way. Whatever you can do or dream you can, begin it. Boldness has genius, power and magic in it. Begin it now."

   - Johann Wolfgang Von Goethe

Michael Jordan

Almost everyone knows Michael Jordan to be the greatest basketball player in the world. When he was a teenager, one year he was not good enough to make the basketball team, but he kept trying. He practiced every day so when his chance came again the next year he would not only make the team, but he would play better than others. One of the reasons he is the greatest is because he probably practices more than any other player. He comes to the gym earlier and stays later than the other players on his team. He practices every day and he knows the value of hard work.

If you want to improve your ability to speak English then you must practice the *10 Secrets* every day. You must speak English every day. You must read aloud every day. You must read aloud and you must read a lot. If you want to be good, you have to pay the price. If you want to speak well, you must practice every day.

My friend Jennifer Wang also loves basketball and plays very well. She likes her English name of Jennifer after Jennifer Rossoti who played for the UCONN Huskies and later played in a professional women's basketball league. Jen Rossoti is not very big, but she is good and she practices a lot too.

Jennifer practices reading aloud almost every day. Many days, early in the morning, I have found Jennifer in the park practicing her English by reading aloud from a book. Some days were very cold and even raining, but she was there practicing anyway. Her English is good enough that she really doesn't need to practice, but she does it anyway. One of the reasons her English is so good is because she practices every day.

If you want to speak well, you must speak every day. If you want to improve your spoken English, you must read aloud every day.

Practice Makes Permanent

One beautiful sunny day, I was walking across campus through the fountains in front of the library. As I passed a young woman sitting on the stairs, I heard her reading aloud. She was practicing, but she was reading so fast that I couldn't understand what she was saying. I walked by and then thought to myself that I should suggest that she slow down. I turned around and went back and said, "Hello, what are you doing." She looked up and with a big smile she said, "Hello, I'm practicing reading English out loud." I complimented her and encouraged her to continue because I told her that it was one of the secrets to improving her spoken English. She seemed very happy to have that reassurance.

Then I asked her, "May I give you a suggestion?" to which she seemed very eager to hear whatever I had to say because I was a foreigner and she could tell that English was my native language. I continued, "I would recommend that when you practice that you read in a very normal speed because you usually speak the same way you practice. When I walked by I knew what you were doing, but I couldn't understand what you were saying because you were speaking so fast." She seemed so pleased that I would take a moment to bring this to her attention and she promised to follow my advice. I also told her that many people believe that practice makes perfect. However, you need to practice correctly because in reality, "practice makes permanent."

Before I walked on, I mentioned that the purpose of speaking is to be understood not just to get the words out. I explained that sometimes the best communication in any language is very slow deliberate speaking so the listener can catch the full impact of the message. For quite a distance down the path, I could her speak the words clearly and could understand exactly what she was saying. I felt like I had made a difference in the life of at least one person.

Life's Paradox

Mary-Jo and I had finished our lunch and prepared to leave for class. I did a last minute check of my e-mail and found the following message from Irene: "To: Dale, Sir. Thank you for your help. Two year before I don't know any English, when I was child instead study English we study Tibetan and Chinese, so I can speak both two language very well. I have three foreign friends, we always play volleyball or go to restaurant, but we can't make a good conversation, because they all can't speak Chinese or Tibetan. When I come here and begin to learn computer, we not only can study English but also can spoke English. It made me very happy! I know you very busy. Our all classmates love you and love your teach. I wish my letter not to disturb you. I am sorry my poor English papers made many mistaken, but I can't do it better. I want make many questions to you, but our class time so short, its very pity. Is represent=stand for? wish=hope? can we say: the thumb stand for the first person the thumb represent the first person? Many happy returns you and your family! From: Cai Rang Zhou Ma"

"Mary-Jo, come quickly!" I called from the living room into the kitchen where she was putting things away. "Oh that's so beautiful," exclaimed Mary-Jo. "It looks like your students love you just like you love them. Oh, you better get going or you'll be late."

"Good afternoon. Is everyone happy?" I cheerfully greeted the class. In unison, they all replied, "Hello, good afternoon. We are happy. Are you happy?" I smiled and said, "I am happy also! Thank you. And thank you Irene for your beautiful message."

I called the roll by looking at the picture cards and carefully saying the person's name and then looking at them so that the written name, my verbalization and visual contact could all help me to get better acquainted with each student and know them individually. Most names were said correctly, but a few students still had to help me with my pronunciation.

"How many of you read the material I gave you last night?" I asked. Every student raised a hand as if to ask for my approval and praise for their obedience and diligence. "That's great! You are very good students and I'm proud of you," I said and then continued, "Did you understand everything you read?" Were there any words that you had difficulty with or that you did not understand after looking them up in the dictionary?" There were several words and phrases that the students asked me about. One by one they were written on the blackboard, explained and discussed and then repeated aloud by the whole class.

After a long pause and a drink of water from my water bottle, I looked over the class and asked, "OK, now let me ask how many of you read the material aloud?" This time only two hands were raised and those came up quite slowly and very timidly as though the students were not sure if they had done the assignment correctly. "Philip, would you like to stand and tell us in your own words the meaning of the first assignment called Paradox of Our Times?" Philip immediately stood and slowly began to read aloud the words on the assignment sheet. I interrupted him and asked him to put the paper down and just in his own words, simple English words, tell the class what he remembers about this reading. He slowly shook his head, shrugged his shoulders and sat down.

"That's OK," I assured Philip and the rest of the class, "I know it is not the custom to read assignments out loud, but unless you do this, your speaking ability will not improve. You will understand what you read, but you will not be able to express your understanding. I want you to read these passages aloud so you can express their meaning in your own words without looking at the text. Perhaps you will need to read the passage several times out loud so you will feel comfortable expressing these ideas in spoken English. If you read them silently, your mind will understand and be comfortable with the words, but your tongue will not. When you read aloud, your brain and your tongue can work together. You will hear yourself say the words and your tongue will be able to repeat them when you speak without reading. It is so very important to read aloud."

I suggested that the class read the passage together aloud. The first time, I would read each sentence and they could repeat it to work on their pronunciation and then they would read the whole homework passage together. They began, Paradox of Our Times, author is anonymous or not known:

1. We have bigger houses, but smaller families; more conveniences, but less time. We have more degrees, but less common sense; more knowledge, but less judgment; more experts, but more problems; more medicine, but less wellness.
2. We spend too recklessly, laugh too little, drive too fast, get angry too quickly, stay up too late, get up too tired; read too little, watch TV too often, and pray too seldom.
3. We have multiplied our possessions, but reduced our values. We talk too much, love too little and lie too often. We've learned how to make a living, but not a life; we've added years to life, not life to years.
4. We have taller buildings, but shorter tempers; wider freeways, but narrower viewpoints. We spend more, but have less; we buy more, but enjoy them less.
5. We've been all the way to the moon and back, but have trouble crossing the street to meet the new neighbor. We've conquered outer space, but not inner space. We've split the atom, but not our prejudice. We write more, but learn less; plan more, but accomplish less.
6. We've learned to rush, but not to wait. We have higher incomes, but lower morals. We build more computers to hold more information, to produce more copies, but have less communication. We are long on quantity, but short on quality.

7. These are the times of fast foods and slow digestion, tall men and short character, steep profits and shallow relationships. We have more leisure and less fun; more kinds of food, but less nutrition; two incomes, but more divorce; fancier houses, but broken homes.

I put the paper down and held up both hands, "All right that was great. Now get a partner and for the next five minutes talk to your partner in English about what that passage means to you. What parts do you remember the best. And don't forget to ask each other questions. Go ahead and begin now." I then went over to sit down on the desk in front of Jane, my dependable co-teacher and translator. "Well Jane, how are we doing? Do you think our system is helping the class? Are the *10 Secrets* working?" She smiled and assured me that she was very pleased and that she wanted to bring her mother to the classes to learn English, but her mother was too shy right now. The class was definitely better than any other English class that she had ever attended.

After the five minutes was over, I got everyone's attention and asked them to read together the other passage called UN 2020 Vision Speech which my wife, Mary-Jo, had given at the Forum on Cooperation Between Anhui and Multi-national Corporations which was held at the Yellow Mountain Resort on October 21-23, 2001. The speech began and everyone again repeated each sentence after me. The speech was as follows:

"Da Giahao. My name is Mary-Jo Christensen and I am a professor at the University of Science & Technology of China located in Hefei City. As I frequently do, I am here representing Dale Christensen, my husband and business partner who was not able to be here because he had a previous engagement in Harbin in northern China. He is a visiting professor teaching in the business school and MBA program of USTC. We both love China with its delicious food, rich culture and history, but most of all, we love the Chinese people.

"Dale sends his greetings, his apologies for not being here and his best wishes to everyone. I'm sure if he were here, he would deliver this speech with greater passion and enthusiasm than I am able. But, in his absence, I will do my best to plant in you the seed of an idea that will capture the hearts and minds of every Chinese person as well as the people of all nations of the earth. It is an idea whose time has come and whose place is here in China!

"First, let me ask you. What is the value of a simple idea? Over the many centuries past, can we begin to measure the power or the expanse of ideas that have moved individuals and nations toward their destinies? It is said that an idea may be more powerful than the strongest army or economic and political force. Such powerful ideas create this strength and guide these forces.

"The world is hungry for such ideas. The idea I am about to share with you will satisfy the largest of appetites; with the promise that China, Anhui Province, Hefei City and the whole world will benefit by its acceptance and implementation. This idea embraces and supports all of China's economic development efforts including APEC, entering the WTO and winning the 2008 Olympic games.

"In preface to describing this idea, I would like to emphasize the dream of China becoming one of, if not the world's greatest leading nation. The question is not if, but when? In order for China to become such, China must be a true leader – leading the way in creativity and innovation – a leader with integrity and a leader with vision.

"This idea's business development plan can initially be written and facilitated by the MBA students at USTC working together with students from all over the globe. This plan is now called UN Vision 2020. This name refers to both the year 2020 and to the term used for 'perfect vision or perfect eyesight'. It describes the development of the 'new home' for the United Nations to be located near Hefei City. I've been told that one translation for the name Hefei means 'where two rivers come together'. What better place is there than here, for all nations to come together. Soon, the Olympics 2008 games will be hosted in Beijing. Tourism will increase dramatically and people from all over the world will come and discover and continue to develop the tremendous opportunities and advantages of doing business here. It is an opportune time for China to extend the invitation for the United Nations to come here and enjoy its long history, rich culture and abundant potential that China has to offer.

By the year 2020, the United Nations City will be the best planned and most modern city on the planet earth. Absent PowerPoint slides of impressive diagrams and beautiful pictures, let your imagination see a magnificent city surrounded by a Great Wall and landscaped with beautiful parks and golf courses, lakes and waterways. This city will include the following:

- A most desirable <u>international airport</u> with flights from all major cities around the world.
- The <u>United Nations capital buildings</u> to be its home for the next 50 to 100 years.
- Various countries <u>consulate offices, housing, office and retail buildings, hotels and restaurants, theaters, churches and museums</u> with each country's unique architecture, decoration and atmosphere.

- A <u>UN University</u> with the best international business and law schools, medical hospital and research center, language institutes and sports stadiums and facilities to host future Olympic games and all kinds of sports including western rodeos, American baseball, ice skating and ice hockey, etc.
- As the <u>world's largest tourist destination</u>, some of the supreme attractions will include the greatest known Disney World, Water World and Zoos, etc. yet to be built and enjoyed.
- The <u>UN Music & Arts Center</u>, will be the next 'Hollywood frontier' of music, art, film, entertainment and culture.
- <u>Adventure and exercise centers</u> for rock climbing, bunji jumping, swimming and weight lifting along with lots of water sports and leisure on the connecting waterways and Lake Chao.

"Visitors will be able to 'tour the world in one city'. The city's infrastructure will include:

- Futuristic elevated rail transportation systems with speed trains and super-highways coming from many major cities. Traffic will be facilitated and controlled as no other city has been able to do before.
- There will be canals, elevators, people movers, walkways, roadways with bike and running trails connecting everything – buildings, airport and sports centers etc.
- This one-of-a-kind city will have traditional, modern, and futuristic architecture and engineering designs of covered and connecting buildings using the best of construction materials with advanced heating, air conditioning and sound systems.

"This city will be the most unique and enviable city in the world. Truly, it will be 'the best of the best' and the 'most desirable city' in which to live. It will attract an unlimited abundance of economic and technological development. This unique city will join with Beijing, Shanghai, Shenzen and Hong Kong as another pillar of power and stability for China and the world. May this idea be planted in your fertile soil and may it take root as you nourish it. And eventually, may it blossom and bear the fruit of unity, peace and prosperity. Thank you very much for your attention."

We all finished together and a few of the students complimented me on these bold and futuristic ideas. They were inspired by them and they seemed appreciative to have been able to have their own imaginations stimulated. I counseled them to read good things that would uplift and build their character. I went on, "Good teachers always emphasize the value of extensive reading. It's through reading many stories and many books that one absorbs the culture, meaning and beauty of the language. So let me say here, 'Read, read, and read!' But, in addition to just reading, read aloud. Reading will help you in many ways, but only reading aloud will help your spoken English. You can read aloud to yourself, to your children, spouse or to other family members. You can even read to your friends or others wanting to learn to speak English. Listening to you read will help them improve their English skills, but they too must read if they want to speak!"

I then taught them that many little children learn to speak by listening to their mothers read to them. I also pointed out that parents learn to read and speak better by reading and speaking to their children. "It's a fact that parents who read to their children are some of the best speakers of their language. Together, both the reader and listener learn to tell stories and add drama and emphasis to words and expressions."

I concluded, "So read to others whenever you can. If there is no one to read to, then read aloud to yourself. Read aloud and read a lot!"

I then gave them a list of good books and authors that would help them get a good feel for the culture of English speaking people as well as give them good exercise in typical English expression. "Don't feel like you need to eat the elephant all in one meal. Pick out a few books that you have access to and begin reading and reading aloud. Make your own list of books to read this next year or over the next few years and enjoy your learning. Remember, it's not a job and it's not something you have to do. It should be something you want to do and that you enjoy. The more you read the more you will enjoy it." I concluded the class with, "Remember, you can eat an elephant one bite at a time!"

Become well read. I suggest the list as follows:

1984
A Christmas Carol
A Connecticut Yankee in King Arthur's Court
A Girl called Liu Yi-ting in Harvard
A Midsummer Night's Dream
A Tale of Two Cities by Charles Dickens
Aesop's Fables
Alice's Adventures in Wonderland
Anna Karenina
Anne of Green Gables
Antony and Cleopatra
Around the World in 80 Days
Autobiography of Thomas Jefferson
Beijingers in New York
Chicken Soup for the Soul
David Copperfield by Charles Dickens

Don Quixote
Dubliners
Emma
Essays (by Bacon)
Essays of Emerson
Fairy Tales by Hans Christian Andersen
Gone With the Wind
Great Expectations
Hamlet
Harry Potter
Ivanhoe
Jane Eyre
Julius Caesar
King Lear
King Solomon's Mines
Last of the Mohicans
Leaves of Grass
Les Miserables
Little Prince
Little Men
Little Women
Lord Jim
Macbeth
Moby Dick
Much Ado About Nothing
Nana (by Emile Zola)
Oliver Twist by Charles Dickens
Othello
Paradise Lost
Paradise Regained
Persuasion
Peter Pan
Poems and Songs of Robert Burns
Poor Richard's Almanac

Pride and Prejudice
Resurrection
Robinson Crusoe
Romeo and Juliet
Sense and Sensibility
Sister Carrie
Short Stories by O. Henry
Stories of Famous People
Tess of the D'Urbervilles
The Adventures of Huckleberry Finn
The Adventures of Pinocchio
The Adventures of Sherlock Holmes
The Adventures of Tom Sawyer
The American Tragedy
The Arabian Nights
The Autobiography (by Benjamin Franklin)
The Call of the Wild
The Catcher in the Rye
The Divine Comedy
The English Patient
The Great Gatsby
The Happy Prince and other Tales
The Holy Bible
The Iliad
The Invisible Man
The Legend of Sleepy Hollow
The Mayor of Casterbridge
The Merchant of Venice
The Mill on the Floss
The Odyssey
The Picture of Dorian Gray
The Pilgrim's Progress
The Portrait of A Lady
The Prince and The Pauper

The Return of Sherlock Holmes
The Return of The Native
The Road Ahead by Bill Gates
The Scarlet Letter
The Sonnets
The Taming of the Shrew
The Wizard of Oz
Twenty Thousand Leagues Under the Sea
Through the Looking Glass
Tom Jones
Treasure Island
Uncle Tom's Cabin
Gulliver's Travels
Ulysses
Vanity Fair
War and Peace
Wuthering Heights

Chapter 6

Call Others on the Telephone

"Would you be excited if someone called you on the telephone and told you that you had just won a million dollars? How excited would you be if all you had to do to win a million dollars was to make a simple telephone call and speak English for 10 minutes so they could understand everything you said and you understood everything they said?"

To Phone or Not To Phone

"How many of you have mobile phones?" was my first question of the day. More than half of the class raised their hands. "How many of you have a telephone in your apartment or dormitory?" I continued. Almost everyone raised a hand. Telephone access and usage in China is experiencing a dramatic increase; however, everyone was aware that there were still hundreds of millions of Chinese people who didn't have easy access to telephones. So how could they call others on the telephone to improve their spoken English? I was determined to help them see that this was not a big problem and encouraged them to discuss any topic.

In my MBA classes, we talk about industry, manufacturing, international business, training, management, environmental issues, education, politics and the economy and so forth. I ask my students, "In comparison to the rest of the world, what is the biggest challenge that China faces today? What do you think is their answer? What is your answer?" I asked the class these questions with an anticipation of hearing something very familiar. I wasn't surprised with what the whole class said almost in unison, "We have too many people!" Then there were ancillary comments about population growth, population control, the one-child policy, opinions about these things and then gradually the comments stopped and there was silence again in the room. I had been listening intently and acknowledged each student's comments during this brief time.

"OK," I said, "Now, what is the greatest asset China has?" With this question, the class didn't respond as quickly. Instead of an almost knee jerk response, they all thought about it and seemed to be weighing several alternatives against each other. But, one by one, they began to respond with things like, "A big market to sell products." "Many people who can help solve problems." And finally, "A large labor force."

I snapped my fingers took several steps forward, "That's right! People! People, lots of people are China's biggest asset. China's biggest problem or liability is also its biggest asset. So, not having a telephone might be a big problem for many wanting to improve their English. But, let me show you how that problem can also be a solution." Then I explained that if you don't have a telephone just stand back to back or sit on the other side of the door in another room and pretend that you're speaking on the telephone. You can have a conversation with someone and not even need to use a telephone. This is also good practice, but then I took them back to using their telephone and calling each other to practice their spoken English. Having a telephone is a big advantage.

No Need for a Native Speaker

Edward raised his hand and asked with enthusiasm, "Can I call you?" "I knew you were going to ask me that question.

Please don't call me, call each other. Remember that I have over 160 MBA students that also want to call me and practice their English. My wife has over 500 students in all of her USTC English classes. If just a few wanted to call every day, we wouldn't have any time to do anything else. Also, keep in mind that in a few weeks when we go home for the summer, I won't be here to practice with. You need to practice with who you can find and who are at the same level of fluency."

Trying to make a natural transition, I explained that many Chinese have the impression that they need to practice with a native English speaker to learn to speak English. I explained, "While it is helpful, it is not absolutely necessary. It's true that children learn to speak English by speaking with adults. However, most of their actual practice speaking is among other children who are learning at their own level. Even babies talk baby talk to one another as they practice their communication skills. Practicing with others at the same level can actually be a very helpful process. It is especially true when you talk to others on the telephone.

"This can be one of the most common and most helpful methods of improving your spoken English," I continued. "First, you must identify others who are willing to speak to you in English on the telephone. These can be your friends, classmates, workmates or family members. You can just call to surprise them or you can make appointments to speak to a number of people every day."

I reminded them that the first few calls may seem very difficult and embarrassing. I advised them not to get discouraged and not to give up! "At first, you may only speak for a few minutes, but as you improve you can spend more time on each call." "The value comes in developing your ability to hear and understand the other person that you cannot see.

You may need to repeat yourself or ask them to repeat what they have said or ask them to speak more slowly." I promised them that very soon, their ear would become accustomed and their speech would also improve so their calling partners would be able to understand them better and they would be able to understand their partners.

I also promised that, "This can be a fun and very useful practice that exercises the many parts of your brain, ear and tongue. Your first calls will seem a little difficult. You may feel a little nervous or awkward. That's normal so don't be afraid. Just go ahead and do it. Perhaps you won't be able to understand what the other person is saying. Remember to be patient and just say, 'I don't understand. Please repeat what you said.' Or 'Please speak more slowly.' Perhaps the other person will not understand you. So you must remember to speak slowly and say your words clearly. If they don't understand you after you have repeated the same thing a few times, then try to say it in a different way. Give them helpful hints so they can grasp your meaning." Remember it's the meaning that you are trying to convey so others understand. You're not just say words or sentences, but you are sharing ideas. Be creative."

What to Say?

One student raised his hand and asked, "How many calls should we make each day or how long should we practice this way?" I answered, "The more you practice, the better you will get and the easier it will be to understand and to be understood. Practicing with the same partner for a short time will help. You will become familiar with each other's voices. However, try to call others and get a variety of experiences and learn to recognize different voices. Men's voices are different from women's voices and they are both different from teenagers and children. The more telephone partners the better. The more people you speak to the better your spoken English will be. Try to find a variety of people who would like to practice speaking English on the telephone with you. Perhaps, in the beginning, you will speak for only a few minutes. Maybe your friends will want to speak for 15 minutes or even longer. Call someone every day. If you can call more than one, that's great! Also, have others call you and begin speaking English right away from the beginning. This will condition your mind to quickly adjust and your tongue to speak naturally. Trust yourself and have confidence. Your mind has the information and your tongue will soon learn to follow. You are just giving them a chance to do what they both do best – to think and to speak – English!"

Another student politely raised her hand and asked, "I want to call others on the telephone, but what can I say?"

"Whatever you want to," I assured her. Then, continuing in an effort to emphasize the importance of doing the activity as being more important than what words you used, I continued, "The more practice the better. If you need a little help to get started, you can find a telephone dialogue in one of your English textbooks. There are hundreds of dialogue books that have many conversation examples in them. You can use them to get started. Study the dialogue before you get on the telephone so you know what you want to say and be able to anticipate what your partner will probably be saying back to you. Practice this before the call, but DO NOT READ YOUR TELEPHONE DIALOGUE! Be sure to practice correctly. Remember, 'Practice doesn't make perfect.' 'Practice makes permanent.' The sooner you get used to speaking on your own, the faster you will progress. If you begin reading your dialogue you won't be talking on the telephone, you will only be reading aloud on the telephone. You may get in the habit and become dependent on reading. It will become a crutch and very soon you will not be able to speak on the telephone without it.

Not completely satisfied with my answer, another student slowly raised her hand and, when I was finished, she repeated the first student's same question, "If we find English speaking partners to make calls, what do we talk about? What words do we say?"

"OK, those are both very good questions," I carefully answered and then asked her in return, "What would you talk about if you were speaking in Chinese or Tibetan? If you don't know what to say in English then just write it down in Chinese or Tibetan and then translate it so you can practice your own dialogue. Say what you are comfortable saying. It will be easier and you will enjoy it more."

The lights seemed to go on in their minds and almost everyone smiled and looked around as if they just realized that this may not be as hard as they thought it would be.

I continued, "Let's practice some customary greetings that people use when talking on the telephone. OK, your partner dials your number and your telephone rings."

Your name is Dong Xu and your friend Xiao Ping is calling you:

Dong Xu, "Hello?"

Xiao Ping, "Hello, this is Xiao Ping."

Dong Xu, "Hi Xiao Ping, this is Dong Xu. How are you?"

Xiao Ping, "I'm fine thank you. And you?"

Dong Xu, "Just fine thanks. What can I do for you?"

Xiao Ping, "I'm calling to see if this is a good time to practice our spoken English. Do you have five or ten minutes to chat?"

Dong Xu, "Oh, I'd love to. I was hoping you would call me today. I have about ten minutes before I have to leave for my appointment. What would you like to talk about?"

Xiao Ping, "Well, today I'm in the mood to talk about sports. Can we talk about the Beijing 2008 Olympics and the next World Cup Football Championship?"

Dong Xu, "Alright, I don't know too much about sports so why don't you tell me about it and I'll ask you some questions. Is that OK?"

Xiao Ping, "I'd love to. Let's start with . . ."

NOTE: Most English textbooks have many telephone dialogues that you can practice with. However, without them, writing your own dialogues is very productive exercise and will help you a lot.

Chapter 7

Group Participation

Synergy: The result of all the parts working together is greater than just the sum of the parts.

There is a mistaken perception by many Chinese people that one must be in a formal class with a foreign teacher to learn to speak English or to participate and practice. This is not the case and those who say you can't learn otherwise are not telling you the truth! Keep in mind that small children progress in their spoken language skills the most when they are speaking to other small children.

A Mute MBA Student

Wang Jiang, one of my MBA students, had studied English for more than ten years. However, when he was asked a question or invited to participate in class, he had great difficulty in speaking. He just couldn't find the words to express himself and he had no self-confidence. When I asked him how his spoken English was, he turned his head and dropped his eyes, raised and waved both hands, and said, "Very poor. Very poor". His classmates laughed and giggled in agreement as though they not only understood, but felt the same way.

"Don't ever say that again," I demanded. "Your English is good. You can speak very well if you want to. Do you want to?" "Yes," he timidly replied. "Then all you have to do is practice and practice – everyday! Will you do it?" He acknowledged that he would. I soon forgot about the encounter until more than a month later, three MBA students invited Mary-Jo and me out to dinner. When we arrived at the restaurant, we met the students, including Wang Jiang. The food was ordered and we enjoyed light conversation, which quickly focused on their recent efforts to improve their spoken English.

Over the past month, they had met together every night from about 6:30 p.m. until about 10:30. During these four hours each evening, they spoke in English and practiced their pronunciation. When asked what they talked about, they explained that they talked about everything from MBA class discussions to international business, politics, religion, families and women. They would just talk and ask each other questions and require explanations about the answers. They would encourage each other and just keep talking until it was time to go home. They did this for one full month and they were now celebrating their success with us.

We were amazed to see the transformation in Wang Jiang and how much he had improved in just one month by just participating in group discussion. He had confidence and participated freely and without hesitation or embarrassment. We were thrilled and complimented him over and over again for his dramatic progress.

English Corners

Throughout China, there are many thousands of people who gather together wanting to improve their spoken English. We all call such a gathering an 'English Corner.' This is a place where people can practice speaking English with each other. Schools, restaurants and hotels have recognized the great demand for such gatherings and have often provided a formal forum for English Corners where students and customers can come to practice English and hopefully add to the company's revenue stream.

These English Corners are valuable and effective. However, they are also costly, not frequent enough and most likely are in a very inconvenient location. Why travel clear across town to pay an expensive fee or buy expensive food in order to speak to someone in English when you could do it for free? Why do it only once a month or once a week when you could do it every day?

You can have your own English Corner every day with two or three friends or occasionally with a larger group. You can also create and teach your own English class. It can be at lunchtime or in the evening or whenever and wherever it's convenient. You can decide and you can make it happen!

Participation Is the Key

When we are children and begin to learn to play football, we first kick the ball a short distance. Over time we learn to kick it harder, faster and with more accuracy. We want to play! We want to be chosen on the team so we can participate and have fun. Those who practice and play the most are usually the ones who become very good at the sport. Those who only watch become spectators and often never learn the real thrill of the game. If they don't play frequently, they either never learn the skills or they gradually lose what they had. So it is with learning to ride a bicycle or learning to swim. Participation is the key! The best way to learn is by doing.

The same principle applies in learning how to speak English. If you are only a spectator and study but never speak then you never develop the speaking skills or you lose what you once had. Participation is the key! You learn to speak by speaking. We gain confidence the more we practice, and the more confidence we have the more we enjoy speaking. The more we enjoy speaking, the more we want to speak. The more we speak, the more confidence and skill we have and so on and so on.

Whether you are in a small group or attend a formal English class at a school, university or language training school, it is vital that you participate. This means that you must ask questions, offer your opinions and actively contribute to the class or group's speaking activities. It's only when you become an active participant that your mind and mouth work together to speak and to improve your speaking ability.

If you remain a passive spectator then your left-brain records what you see and hear while your right brain weakens and speaking difficulty increases. Also, remember that you cannot participate if you do not attend. Be an active and dedicated member of your group or class. As you participate, you are practicing many of the skills necessary to increase verbal speech.

World Cup Cheerleaders

One day, in the Tibetan Spoken English class, we talked about the previous day's football game between China and Costa Rica. Thinking that if a small country like Senegal could defeat the great French world champions by a score of 1-0, then China could certainly win their match too. I had predicted a score of 3 to 1 in favor of China. But, along with a third of the world's population, I was disappointed to see them lose.

During the discussion, someone asked, "What do you call those who make lots of noise?"

"Oh, you mean those who cheer?" I asked in return. As I wrote on the blackboard and slowly repeated to the class several times, "They are called cheerleaders." And, "They are also called the cheer team." I had the class repeat the sentences several times and made sure everyone understood. Jane repeated the sentences in Chinese, but there was no need because everyone was nodding their heads that they understood.

Then I asked the class, "What do cheerleaders do? What is their purpose?"

Everyone thought carefully. It was Irene who first said, "They encourage the team."

"That's right. They encourage the team," I repeated several times as I wrote beneath the other words on the blackboard. "What does encourage mean?," I asked.

Someone said, "They give the team courage."

"Yes, they give the team courage. Let's repeat that several times." I said the word 'courage' and used it in some sentences and they repeated after me what I had said. People down the hall could hear the strong duplicated cadence of Courage. Encourage. I have courage. You have courage. She has courage. He has courage. They have courage. I encourage you. You encourage me. He encourages her. They encourage us, and so on.

"What else do they do?" I asked. No one seemed to have any more answers so I offered and then wrote, "They involve the fans. What does 'involve' mean?" The same process was followed to make sure everyone knew what involve, involving and involvement meant. Someone looked in their electronic dictionary and shouted out, "Participate!" "Yes, that's right!" I beamed with encouragement. Then they did the same for participate, participating and participation.

"What else do cheer leaders do?" I continued.

Quickly and with his big happy smile, Cari raised his hand and said, "They help their team to win."

"That's great!" I agreed and wrote, "They help their team to win." Then, turning towards the class I had them repeat after me, "I help you to win. You help me to win. He helps her win. She helps them to win. We help them to win," and so on.

"What else? Can anyone think of something else that cheer leaders do?" This time there was a much longer silence, as the students seemed to struggle in thought to come up with an answer. It was difficult to respond this way. From past experience they knew if I asked them a question there must be an answer. But, they just couldn't seem to think of any. After what seemed like a long time, someone confidently said with a smile, "I don't know. Please tell me."

"Good response," I said in an encouraging way as I turned to the blackboard and wrote and continued to speak. "Cheerleaders entertain the TV audience." Then the familiar dialogue ritual was repeated for entertain, entertaining and entertainment using many sentences. Everyone repeated the words and sentences after me as if they were buying them from me. I went on to explain that entertainment meant enjoyment and making something interesting.

Once they repeated them and said them out loud, it was like they now owned them. These words and sentences were theirs and they could use them when they wanted. They could teach or sell them to others just as I had shared with them. They were no longer the students, but they were English teachers with confidence and skill. They knew their English wasn't perfect, but they also knew that neither was their Chinese perfect nor was their Tibetan. They liked speaking and teaching English and they were improving. That was what was important. Progression not perfection is the key to speaking English.

I turned to my eager audience. "Let me ask you this, 'Am I a cheerleader?'" With chalk all over my hands, I paused a long time before going on as I looked into each their faces. One by one they began to smile and say, "Yes, you are a cheerleader." "That's right, I am a cheerleader. You are a cheerleader. We are cheerleaders." Everyone repeated after me in a happy rhythm.

Then I emphasized my point as I said more slowly and pointed to each line under what cheerleaders do, "Teachers encourage their class. Teachers involve the students. Teachers help the students to speak English. Teachers entertain the students by making English fun and interesting. Teachers are cheerleaders!" Again in unison they began, "I am a cheerleader, you are a cheerleader, we are cheerleaders . . ."

Everyone seemed to be enjoying this new perspective on teaching when Jane asked, "What do the cheerleaders say when they cheer?"

"Good question. Does everyone understand the question? Let's repeat it," and they did. I wrote the word CHINA in big capital letters on the blackboard. "Give me a C!" I roared as I pointed to the "C" in China.

Almost as if they had been practicing for a long time, they all answered "C!" Give me an "I!" "I!" Give me an "N!" "N!" Give me an "A!" "A!" What do you have?" I shouted. "China!" was the answer. Everyone laughed and clapped as if they had just won the world cup.

"OK, let's turn to your partner and talk for three minutes about teaching spoken English," I instructed as I apologized for having to leave the class early and go to my 2:00 p.m. appointment. I could hear them practicing as I walked down the hall and got on the elevator on the sixth floor. "Why not create a teacher's cheer," I thought to myself. "This way they can really cheer their students along." Feeling almost like a high school student at heart, I began to form the following words in my mind:

1   2   3   4   -   1   2   3   4
We are teachers! Hen hao teachers!
We speak English! Hen hao English!

How to do it! We can teach you!
Do the secrets! To speak English!

Every day now! All 10 Secrets!
Every day now! You speak English!

Give me an S!
Give me a P!
Give me an E!
Give me an A!
Give me a K!

And what have you got? S   P   E   A   K!

What do you do? SPEAK!

(Yay ! ! ! ! Applaud ! ! ! !)

"*Speak what?*"
"*Speak English!*"

"That's great," I said as I picked up my briefcase and headed for the door. "Now you can teach your students that. 'What do we speak?'" I shouted. "We speak English!" the class roared back. I waved and everyone waved back as they bid farewell for another day.

Chapter 8

Interpret for Others

"The truth of the matter is that there's nothing you can't accomplish if: (1) You clearly decide what it is that you're absolutely committed to achieving, (2) You're willing to take massive action, (3) You notice what's working or not, and (4) You continue to change your approach until you achieve what you want, using whatever life gives you along the way."
- Anthony Robbins

Anyone, Any Time, Any Place

You can interpret for anyone, any time and in any place. Interpreting is one of the strongest methods of exercising your whole brain to improve your speaking ability. You are forced to draw on your left-brain reserves while you exercise your right brain skills. It is similar to teaching others, but even more powerful because you have to hear in Chinese, mentally understand and translate information in your mind and almost instantly verbalize these ideas correctly into English.

The more advanced your English speaking ability is, the better interpreter you are. It only stands to reason that you should begin to interpret a lot very early in your study of the English language. Don't wait until you are proficient in speaking and then learn to interpret.

Keep in mind that interpreting is not translating written documents. That is another very different skill involving mostly the left-brain. On the one hand, it is mostly a skill requiring good visual and writing abilities. On the other hand anyone can translate spoken English without knowing how to read or write. Little children are some of the best translators and teachers because they are focused on speaking and communicating meaning. You can do it also!

What Do You See?

After the class warm-up exercises, it was Badun's (Wan Ma) turn to begin the first exercise. "Badun, would you please interpret for Dylan (Yong Chun Cao)?" I asked. From years of obediently following their teacher's instructions, Badun and Dylan both stood to do whatever was asked of them.

"I have never interpreted before," Badun explained. "Oh that's OK, it's easy, I reassured him. Dylan is going to speak in Tibetan and you tell me whatever he says." Both stood frozen and unable to continue. Badun continued, "What if I can't say the words?" "That's OK too. Just try to convey to me the meaning of what he says. Don't worry about trying to translate every word. Just listen to him and when you understand his meaning then just do your best to describe it to me in English."

Now, all eyes were on Dylan. He looked like he felt trapped in a corner and didn't know how to escape. "Go ahead Dylan," I directed. "Say anything you want in Tibetan or Chinese and Badun will interpret for you and tell me what you have said." Dylan just didn't seem to know what to talk about. His mind was frozen and he had no idea where to begin. One by one, the other students began to whisper suggestions in Tibetan. This seemed to confuse him even more. Then I offered to help, "Dylan, look out the window and tell Badun what you see." Then, along with the whole class, he turned to look out the window and began, "I see trees and . . ." I interrupted, "No," "you must speak in Tibetan or Chinese. Tell Badun what you see in Tibetan so he can interpret for you in English. Now go ahead. What do you see out the window?"

Dylan began to speak in beautiful Tibetan words and I stopped him after several sentences. "OK, Badun. What did he say?" Badun seemed unsure of how to continue as he stumbled over the words, "He said he sees trees." "What kind of trees? Big trees? Little trees? What color are the trees? Go ahead and ask him," I commanded as I turned my back to the window and only looked at Baden. He quickly passed the message and Dylan responded in like manner so Baden could explain to me, "He sees beautiful trees. Some are large and some are very small. They are all green trees."

"Good," I snapped back. "What else does he see? Ask him what else he sees out the window." Again there was a flurry of unfamiliar words back and forth and again Baden turned to me to explain that Dylan saw some buildings. "What kind of buildings?" I asked. "Are they large buildings? How many? What color are they? How big are they? Go ahead. Ask him to tell us about the buildings."

The answers came back and soon everyone had a clear image of the sky and clouds, trees, bicycles and buildings and students. The whole class seemed very pleased with the quality of translation that Badun had done. As he sat down, he seemed pleased with himself and I complimented him on painting a beautiful picture with his words.

How Do You Feel? What do you like? What do you like to do? What Do You Wish?

"That's how you translate," I explained. "You don't need a foreign speaker. You can translate for each other. The more you practice, the better your speaking ability will be. You can talk about things you see or how you feel. You can describe the things you like or don't like. You can also play a game called 'Make A Wish'. For example, if you had a magic wand and could wave it and make things just like you want, what would you wish for? Then describe whatever your imagination sees or whatever you want."

The class divided up into groups of three and everyone took a turn as interpreter, English speaker and native speaker. The assignment was given to practice this type of exercise every day with each other or to actually interpret for others throughout the day. The instructions were given to look for opportunities to interpret and to make opportunities to interpret.

A Beautiful Description

Later that night, when I arrived home and checked my e-mail, I found the following beautiful message from Irene (Cai Rang Zhuo Ma):

To: Dale, Hi dale, How are you? Let me tell your daughter about Tibet. In Tibet all people believed in Buddhism, especially the old. They pray whole day, even if they eating. Tibetan likes sing and dance, everyone can do it when they meet wedding ceremony or another patty, All people sing and dance in a circle. Even their are doing job. For example, the herdsman sing with ride, the children sing the way to go to school, women cook with sing.

At the Spring Festival or Tibetan holiday, people will wear their best dresses and all jewelry, bring a long white strips of silk called khatag to visit the honored people or the old. The khatag is the symbol of honor, like the dragon symbol of the fortunate and satisfying in Tibet. Tibetan people continue have many old customs. For example, they like long hair women usually made hair to one braid, two braids even hundreds slim braids. You can see many woman's braids swimming up the legs. Maybe you will meet man who also braided and carried beautiful knife. Don't surprise. It's only a decoration.

We all like to eat meat (not pork) and tsamba. The tsamba make from highland barley. People parched it to be ripe, smashed it to be powder. when we want to eat ,we put sugar, butter and some another flavorings to a bowl. then poured hot tea, when the flavoring dissolve. put tsamba in the bowl, mixed these to a tower. It's has plentiful nutrition and special tasty. You can eat tsamba with milk, tea or another drink.

Most Tibetan lived on the plateau (tableland), so they had bad condition. no water and resource less, but people enjoy there. From: Irene

Interpreting is merely conveying in a second language what one understands or sees in their mind as they listen to the words of the first language. It may be helpful to merely look at it as a way of describing things that you are listening to. Do it and do it often (every day) and your spoken English will improve dramatically.

Chapter 9

Memorize New Words & Phrases

> *"I believe the single most significant decision I can make on a day-to-day basis is my choice of attitude . . . When my attitudes are right, there is no barrier too high, no valley too deep, no dream too extreme, no challenge too great for me."*
>
> \- Charles Swindoll

Try New Things

"What do Americans eat for breakfast?" was the class's first question. I described a typical breakfast of hot or cold cereal with toast and jam, orange juice and milk. Then I described to the class my favorite breakfast of eggs (scrambled, omelet, medium cooked sunny side up) hash browns and bacon with a side order of pancakes or French-toast. I wrote everything on the blackboard and the students copied everything in their notebooks. When we were all finished writing, there were lots of hungry looks. I was even imagining these delicious things in my mind when a student asked, "What are pancakes and French toast?" Another student then raised her hand and asked, "What are hash browns and bacon?"

After spending almost fifteen minutes carefully explaining how to prepare each and drawing lots of pictures on the blackboard, I realized that still no one really knew what I was talking about. I asked, "How would you like to come to my house tomorrow for class. My wife will fix us pancakes, French toast, hash browns and bacon so you can all see it, taste it and know what Americans like to eat for breakfast?" There was an instantaneous applause and excited agreement from all the students.

"OK, I'll make the arrangement. You should eat your lunch before coming. Mary-Jo will only be able to make enough for everyone to have a taste of everything, but not enough for a whole meal. Is that alright?" Everyone agreed that this was the best thing so our class wouldn't become a burden for her.

The next day, promptly at 1:00 p.m., the students knocked at our door and we ushered them all into our small living room where we had about 15 seats arranged around two small tables. Not all the students had come because several had returned to their hometowns to take an examination and wouldn't return for some time. Everyone there was excited and began to comment on the delicious smells in the air as they looked around the room and complimented us on the pictures of our family etc. They were particularly interested in knowing who the picture of the young man with the beard was. I told them his name was Jesus Christ and that we were Christians. They were so very respectful and asked many questions. I was able to answer some of them, but told them that I was not able to answer all of their questions right now. They were hungry for more when Mary-Jo showed up with the first two plates of pancakes with butter and syrup all cut up for them to taste with their toothpicks.

Everyone loved it and wanted more so she made more. Then in a few minutes she came out with two plates of French toast and bacon which was enthusiastically received. As the students tasted these new things, I explained that Americans liked this sweet breakfast. The students all practiced their English by commenting, "What is this? This is a pancake. I like pancake. I like to eat pancakes. I like French toast. This is bacon. I like bacon very much." And "Thank you for the pancake." Then came the hash browns and the students soon learned that the toothpicks didn't work very well. Before Mary-Jo could bring in the chop sticks the students were eating them with their fingers.

The students were curious about many western things and I just answered one question after another until someone suggested that class was over and they should go. They politely thanked us for our hospitality and excused themselves. One by one they found their shoes among the many pairs outside our front door and waved goodbye as they walked down the stairs.

The Money

The next day in class, there arose a lengthy discussion about the student's desire to pay me for my teaching. I told them I had long ago fallen in love with all of them and I was not teaching them for money. The experiment was working. They were learning to speak English using the 10 Secrets and I was thrilled just to be there. Nevertheless, they insisted on trying to raise money and solicit support from the Trace Foundation that helped them come to USTC.

I insisted that if they had money, we should use it for a party or a nice dinner or something that everyone could enjoy. I had been compensated enough and I wouldn't accept any money. It was agreed and we went on with the class.

Start With What You Need

In order to progress in learning to speak English, it is vital that you add new words to your vocabulary. Perhaps there are words assigned or those you desire to learn. It always helps to have a small list of words that you are referring to in order to master them. However, remember that the only way you can truly master them is to use them in everyday speech and conversation. Only when you speak the words in sentences will you own them. If you faithfully do this over a period of a few years, your vocabulary will be as large as most native English speakers.

Generally speaking, Chinese people have a huge English vocabulary in their mind, but cannot use it in speaking. Begin now to learn, memorize and use new words every day.

Also, memorizing quotes and phrases is similar to adding new vocabulary words. But, instead of just words, you add entire sentences to your speaking ability. When you begin adding quotes and phrases to your "vocabulary" and then use them in your speech, you are making great progress in your ability to speak English. Remember, don't just memorize them in your mind. Use them in your everyday speaking. Speak! Speak! Speak!

Example Phrases To Memorize (Make Categories or Topic Headings)

The following quotes will help you get started on their own list. You can make a list and choose the ones you like and begin today to memorize new words and phrases:

Attitude

"One person with a belief is worth more than a hundred who are merely interested."
- Anonymous

"A reputation once broken may possibly be repaired, but the world will always keep their eyes on the spot where the crack was."
- Joseph Hall

"Make sure your words match your deeds."
- Ed Kugler

"We're only as big as the smallest thing that can divert us from our goal."
- Jim Stovall

"Make sure where you're headed is where you want to be!"
- Ed Kugler

"The weak can never forgive. Forgiveness is the attribute of the strong."
- Ghandi

"The key to your future is YOU."
- Ed Kugler

"Make sure your ideals are worth living up to."
- Ed Kugler

"Time is more valuable than money. You can get more money but you can't get any more time."
- Jin Rohn

"Make sure you know what you're trading your time for ... and that it's worth it."
- Ed Kugler

"Knowledge is power ... only when it is applied."
- Ed Kugler

"The key to your future is you."
- Ed Kugler

"He who kneels before God can stand before anyone."
- Anonymous

"We must first overcome ourselves to make any progress as a human being."
- Ed Kugler

"There is no convenient time to render service to another."
- Ed Kugler

"The same wind blows on everyone ... the set of the sail will make all the difference in your life's fortunes."
- Jim Rohn

"We cannot always build the future for our youth, but we can build our youth for the future."
- Franklin D. Roosevelt

"Don't ask what your country can do for you, but ask what you can do for your country."
- John F. Kennedy

"Education is what remains after one has forgotten everything he learned in school."
- Anonymous

"Give a man a fish and you feed him for a day. Teach a man to fish and you feed him for a lifetime."
- Anonymous

"Faith is the cornerstone on which all great lives are built."
- Anonymous

"It is not who you once were but, who you are and what you may become."
- Anonymous

"To do anything truly worth doing, I must not stand back shivering and thinking of the cold and danger, but jump in with gusto and scramble through as well as I can."
- Og Mandino

"The spirit, the will to win, and the will to excel are the things that endure. These qualities are so much more important than the events that occur."
- Vince Lombardi

"Nothing can stop the man with the right mental attitude from achieving his goal; nothing on earth can help the man with the wrong mental attitude."
- Thomas Jefferson

"Our greatest glory is not in never falling, but in rising every time we fall."
- Confucius

"The will to win, the desire to succeed, the urge to reach your full potential . . . these are the keys that will unlock the door to personal excellence."
- Eddie Robinson

"EARN as much as you can. SAVE as much as you can. INVEST as much as you can. GIVE as much as you can."
- Reverend John Wellesly

"Take care of your body with steadfast fidelity. The soul must see through these eyes alone, and if they are dim, the whole world is clouded."
- Johann Wolfgang Von Goethe

"One of life's most painful moments comes when we must admit that we didn't do our homework, that we are not prepared."
- Merlin Olsen

"The person who knows HOW will always have a job. The person who knows WHY will always be his boss."
- Diane Ravitch

"I love the man who can smile in trouble, who can gather strength from distress, and grows brave by reaction. 'Tis the business of little minds to shrink, but he whose heart is firm, and whose conscience approves his conduct, will pursue his principles unto death."
- Thomas Paine

"The great blessings of mankind are within us and within our reach."
- Seneca

"If you have a positive attitude and constantly strive to give your best effort, eventually you will overcome your immediate problems and find you are ready for greater challenges."
- Pat Riley

"We will either find a way, or make one."
- Hannibal

"Ability is what you're capable of doing. Motivation determines what you do. Attitude determines how well you do it."
- Lou Holtz

"Life affords no higher pleasure than that of surmounting difficulties, passing from one step of success to another, forming new wishes and seeing them gratified."
- Samuel Johnson

"Happiness, like unhappiness, is a proactive choice."
- Stephen R. Covey

"If you have a positive attitude and constantly strive to give your best effort, eventually you will overcome your immediate problems and find you are ready for greater challenges."
- Pat Riley

"Ability is what you're capable of doing. Motivation determines what you do. Attitude determines how well you do it."
   - Lou Holtz

"Keep away from small people who try to belittle your ambitions. Small people always do that, but the really great make you feel that you, too, can become great."
   - Mark Twain

"If you have one true friend you have more than your share."
   - Thomas Fuller

"In the end, the only people who fail are those who do not try."
   - David Viscott

"The way for a young man to rise is to improve himself in every way he can, never suspecting that anybody wishes to hinder him."
   - Abraham Lincoln

"Efficient management is doing things right; effective leadership is doing the right things."
   - Peter F. Drucker

"Remember, success is not measured by heights attained but by obstacles overcome."
   - Bruce Jenner

"A great attitude does much more than turn on the lights in our world; it seems to magically connect us to all sorts of serendipitous opportunities that were somehow absent before the change."
   - Earl Nightingale

"Do not follow where the path may lead. Go, instead, where there is no path and leave a trail."
   - Anonymous

"If your dream is a big dream, and if you want your life to work on the high level that you say you do, there's no way around doing the work it takes to get you there."
- Joyce Chapman

"Nothing is impossible; there are ways that lead to everything, and if we had sufficient will we should always have sufficient means. It is often merely for an excuse that we say things are impossible."
- Francis de La Rochefoucauld

"Faith is an oasis in the heart which will never be reached by the caravan of thinking."
- Kahlil Gibran

"You gain strength, courage, and confidence by each experience in which you really stop to look fear in the face. You are able to say to yourself, 'I have lived through this horror. I can take the next thing that comes along. You must do the thing you think you cannot do."
- Eleanor Roosevelt

"The battle of life is, in most cases, fought uphill; and to win it without a struggle were perhaps to win it without honor. If there were no difficulties there would be no success; if there were nothing to struggle for, there would be nothing to be achieved."
- Samuel Smiles

"You cannot always control what goes on outside. But you can always control what goes on inside."
- Wayne Dyer

"You don't learn to hold your own ground in the world by standing on guard, but by attacking and getting well hammered yourself."
- George Bernard Shaw

"People in their handlings of affairs often fail when they are about to succeed. If one remains as careful at the end as he was at the beginning, there will be no failure."

- Lao-Tzu

"Continuous, unflagging effort, persistence and determination will win. Let not the man be discouraged who has these."

- James Whitcomb Riley

"Our real problem, then, is not our strength today; it is rather the vital necessity of action today to ensure our strength tomorrow."

- Dwight D. Eisenhower

"If something is wrong, fix it if you can. But train yourself not to worry. Worry never fixes anything."

- Mrs. Ernest Hemingway

"It is necessary for us to learn from others' mistakes. You will not live long enough to make them all yourself."

- Hyman G. Rickove

"Begin doing what you want to do now. We are not living in eternity. We have only this moment, sparkling like a star in our hand — and melting like a snowflake."

- Marie Beyon Ray

"You can give without loving, but you cannot love without giving."

- Amy Carmichael

"I believe that anyone can conquer fear by doing the things he fears to do, provided he keeps doing them until he gets a record of successful experience behind him."

- Eleanor Roosevelt

"There is no sense in crying over spilt milk. Why bewail what is done and cannot be recalled?"
 - Sophocles

"We can't afford to waste tears on might-have-beens. We need to turn the tears into sweat that can take us to what can be."
 - Denis Waitley

"If you want to achieve excellence, you can get there today. As of this second, quit doing less-than-excellent work."
 - Thomas J. Watson

"The first thing I do in the morning is to make my bed and while I am making up my bed I am making up my mind as to what kind of a day I am going to have."
 - Robert Frost

"First say to yourself what you would be; and then do what you have to do."
 - Epictetus

"Handle them carefully, for words have more power than atom bombs."
 - Pearl Strachan Hurd

"There is one thing stronger than all the armies in the world, and that is an idea whose time has come."
 - Victor Hugo

"Life is too short to waste. Dreams are fulfilled only through action, not through endless planning to take action."
 - David J. Schwartz

"I will greet this day with love in my heart. For this is the greatest secret of success in all ventures . . . my love will melt all hearts like unto the sun whose rays soften the coldest day."
 - Og Mandino

"When you want to encourage a greater sense of responsibility in others (and yourself), emphasize the anticipation of accomplishment, not the penalties for failure."

- Roger Crawford

"What you possess in the world will be found at the day of your death to belong to someone else. But what you are will be yours forever."

- Henry Van Dyke

"The last three or four reps is what makes the muscle grow. This area of pain divides the champion from someone else who is not a champion. That's what most people lack, having the guts to go on and just say they'll go through the pain no matter what happens."

- Arnold Schwarzenegger

"Character cannot be developed in ease and quiet. Only through experiences of trial and suffering can the soul be strengthened, vision cleared, ambition inspired and success achieved."

- Helen Keller

"Pure love is a willingness to give without a thought of receiving anything in return."

- Peace Pilgrim

"The hero and the coward both feel the same thing, but the hero uses his fear, projects it onto his opponent, while the coward runs. It's the same thing, fear, but it's what you do with it that matters."

- Gus D'Amato

"We are continually faced by great opportunities brilliantly disguised as insoluble problems."

- Lee Iococca

"Don't tell your problems to people: eighty percent don't care; and the other twenty percent are glad you have them."
- Lou Holtz

"When we are motivated by goals that have deep meaning, by dreams that need completion, by pure love that needs expressing, then we truly live life."
- Greg Anderson

"The greater part of our happiness or misery depends on our dispositions and not our circumstances."
- Martha Washington

"We must not, in trying to think about how we can make a big difference, ignore the small daily differences we can make which, over time, add up to big differences that we often cannot foresee."
- Marian Wright Edelman

"Remind yourself regularly that you are better than you think you are. Successful people are not superhuman. Success does not require a super intellect. Nor is there anything mystical about success. And success isn't based on luck. Successful people are just ordinary folks who have developed belief in themselves and what they do. Never – yes – never sell yourself short."
- David J. Schwartz

"The price of success is hard work, dedication to the job at hand, and the determination that whether we win or lose, we have applied the best of ourselves to the task at hand."
- Vince Lombardi

"When you really love something the first thing you want to do is share it!"
- Ed Pineger

"There are depths in the sea which the storms that lash the surface into fury never reach. They who reach down into the depths of life where, in the stillness, the voice of God is heard, have the stabilizing power which carries them poised and serene through the hurricane of difficulties."
- Spencer W. Kimball

"Nothing is as strong as gentleness or as gentle as strength."
- Anonymous

Chapter 10

Read, Write, and Memorize Poetry

"Words do not only convey meaning, they call them forth."
- David O. McKay

"Poetry restores to words their power to evoke presence."
- Marcel

What is poetry?

I handed out the gift I had prepared for each of my Tibetan students. It was a simple copy of my small book of poetry titled *Thoughts In Verse* that I had written over the past thirty years. I read to them the first poem titled "Truth Is Like An Apple" and then one by Edgar A. Guest called "Wisdom". Everyone seemed excited and was very thankful. Politely, they all asked me to write my signature on the title page. One by one, I signed them and explained that some poems may be better than others. I also promised them that if they daily read, wrote and memorized poetry, their spoken English would improve.

Then, walking to the center of the class, I stood with both hands on the podium making eye contact with one student after another. I continued with my own thoughts, "Like music, poetry enlightens the soul while it exercises the mind in rhythm and vivid imagery. By reading, writing and memorizing poetry, you are exercising one of the highest forms of spoken English. It energizes both the left and right sides of the brain while it conditions your thinking and trains your tongue."

"What is poetry?" I asked the class. No one seemed to have an answer. "OK, I think poetry is just normal language used in the most efficient manner to express simple things in the most profound and beautiful way. It's a way of packing the most meaning into the least number of words and having them sound like a song." Everyone looked at me and at each other so I turned to Jane and asked her to help translate. With her brief explanation everyone seemed to agree and be delighted with the definition. "The one big difference between poetry and other forms of writing is that poetry usually has a rhythm to it and the words at the end of the sentences usually rhyme with each other. Does anyone know what the word 'rhythm' or 'rhyme' means?" Again, no one seemed to understand so Jane again quickly explained and they all began to chatter to each other in Tibetan and Chinese and repeat the word 'rhyme' and 'rhythm'. They knew these words, but hadn't recognized them when I had first said them.

Again, I leaned forward with my elbows on the podium and said, "You may not believe this, but when I was a young man, I was not able to speak English very well at all. I didn't read much and I didn't talk much unless I was mad." Everyone laughed. "It was about the time when I was sixteen years old that I was introduced to secret number ten, and it helped me to improve my spoken English very much. In fact, I think that this has been one of the things that has probably helped me the most to verbally express myself." There was kind of a soft "Ohhh" or "Ahhh" sound from the whole class as if to say, "That's how you do it."

I then continued, "When I was in high school, one of my English teachers introduced poetry to us and told us about 'iambic pentameter'. Kind of like 'Da, dA, dA, Da, Da, dA, dA, Da.'" I wrote this on the blackboard and while continuing to speak and chanting the beat. "Now, I won't try to go into detail, but it means a kind of rhythm. There are many kinds of rhythms to poetry and this is only one of them." Everyone seemed very confused because they had never heard or seen these words. Again, Jane came to the rescue to quickly explain the idea so I could continue. "Remember, reading and memorizing other people's poetry is enjoyable and will help improve your spoken English. But, also remember that writing and memorizing your own poetry will help you in a way that nothing else can. When you try it, you will see what I mean."

With a fresh new piece of chalk in my hand and with a broad sweep of my arm, in a gesture that a magician would make, I spun around toward the blackboard and said, "Are you ready! Great! Let's try a few simple poems to give you the idea. I call this one 'My 4 Favorite Colors.'" I wrote on the blackboard:

Grasses are green, and skies are blue;
Sunshine warms me, and so do you.

The class must have understood and really liked it, because they reacted like a group of small children just offered a special treat. "Let's try another one. This next one, I call 'Young At Heart,'" I continued as I began to write again:

As hand in hand we go along,
  enjoying life together,
May we always sing a song,
  and stay young at heart forever.

Oh yes, they really liked that one. It had a touch of romance and they all could relate to that. "You know, many of the poems I have written over the years, I have written for my wife, Mary-Jo. This next one, I wrote for her many years ago and titled it 'Tribute To My Wife'". I didn't explain to the class, but I remembered that it was her love of my poetry that helped me to identify her as that special one whom I had been looking for to be my wife. After a long pause, I very carefully and thoughtfully wrote in big letters for all to see:

To a Goddess of beauty, a modern Helen of Troy,
A lover of poetry, a source of great joy.

Without my request, Jane quickly translated and explained the words and the mythical character, Helen of Troy, that she knew they would not be familiar with. Everyone seemed to be enchanted by this newfound thing called poetry, "English poetry". It seemed to make learning to speak English an art rather than a science. They were beginning to discover and to understand the real power of the *10 Secrets*. How could it be that the rest of the world didn't know about this? Oh, so many Chinese people try so hard and are not able to do what they want to do so badly. So many are not able to tap into their own knowledge and resources that they have worked so hard to develop. What a pity.

It seemed almost as if I could read their minds and know exactly what they were feeling. With my eyes, I tried to pierce their very hearts. "I know that every one of you has a strong desire to improve your spoken English. You have a dream to speak as you hear and see me speak. Even though you may not be as good as you want to be, your English is very good. You are making great progress. I can see it better than you can see it yourself. OK, maybe right now you feel like a worm and you can only awkwardly crawl on the ground. But, if you keep working and trying and developing your confidence and skills, you will someday be able to fly like the wind. You will speak with grace and ease. You can and will do it! I know you can do it!"

I stopped and took the time to look into each student's face and acknowledge, eye to eye, that what I said was possible. No words were exchanged, only feeling and assurance that they were on their way. So often I tried to teach them that words are only one way of communication. The eye contact and the body language will sometimes communicate more meaning than words can ever describe. This was such a moment and everyone heard me loud and clear.

What seemed like just the right moment, I stood erect and with my book of poetry in hand, I read the following poem titled "The Ugly Caterpillar":

Life's days oft make us, one and all,
  bend in anguish to a crawl;
Like the caterpillar innate to be, a
  butterfly so swift and free.
When in our heart there's pain and hurt,
  all we see is grass and dirt.
How we long to upward fly,
  enjoying high views from the sky.
But, tightly a cocoon we 'round us fold,
  against harsh winds so bitter cold.
While the desire to live we slowly kill,
  in this jacket so quiet and still.
There we could stay and wither up,
  not drinking from life's bitter cup;
Always unhappy and in a fuss,
  refusing what life has to offer us.
While nature's springing the pangs of growth,
  troubled by warmth that's shared by both;
Cause us to stir and squirm about,
  struggling hard and worming out.
The moment we think the battle's lost,
  desire's value surmounts all cost.
For in a moment when our tears are dry,
  we'll find ourselves a butterfly.

"Now that we have read that, let's try to write a little poetry, shall we?" I asked the class. No one moved thinking this was something like an examination that they had not prepared for. "It's not so hard," I reassured them. "What shall we write about? Come on give me some topics." Someone said, "Romance". Another student said, "A tiger." After a long pause, someone offered, "Why not a drink of water?"

I wrote the three words on the board – Romance, Tiger, Water. "Ok let's give it a try I tried to say with confidence," Let's look at the words as an artist would look at his canvas and paints or a sculptor would look at a piece of stone he was about to chisel on. I wrote a line or two and then erased a few words and replaced them with new ones. After a few minutes, I was finished and stepped back for everyone to see. They all read together the following poem:

I feel like a tiger when I'm away from you.
I am so very thirsty, and feel very blue.
Your kisses are like water, refreshing and divine.
Won't you come and kiss me, so you can then be mine.

Everyone cheered and said, "Can we try again!" "Sure," I replied. "What shall we write about?" Ben raised his hand and with a smile said, "Tibet, let's write about beautiful Tibet." "That's a great idea. Anything else? What about Tibet? What do you want to write about?" They thought for a few minutes and then William said, "Mutton, I like to eat mutton." The word mutton was written beneath the word Tibet. "I like to drink barley wine," said Badun. "I like to eat Tsamba," said Helen. The words were written on the blackboard with the others and I went to work as I had done before and again I turned to read with the class the following:

When I dream of home, homesick I often get.
I long to see the mountains, and to visit my Tibet.
I love to eat the mutton, and drink the barley wine.
Play the music and the dances, and the Tsamba is so fine.
My family will be happy, to see how much I've grown.
I'll have so much to tell them, when I will soon go home.

Later, someone in the class corrected me and explained that the word I thought sounded like "mutton" didn't mean sheep, but in the Tibetan language it meant butter. They all were very pleased. I then explained that another kind of poetry could be called lyrics without rhyme. Before reading the thoughts I had written earlier I said, "The following describes what a foreigner feels about China:"

When I see through your eyes,
  I see the beauty and ugliness of life.
    When I walk in your shoes,
  I understand your history and future dreams.
When I eat your food,
  I feel your hunger and satisfaction.
    When I speak your language,
  I appreciate your joy and sadness.
When I live among you,
  I become one with you.

"Ahhh," sighed the class in unison. "That is beautiful."

Poems To Practice With

Then I explained that everyone was free to find and choose their own poetry. They could practice reading the poems I had given them earlier titled "The Ugly Caterpillar", "Truth Is Like An Apple", and a few short ones along with "Wisdom" by Edgar A. Guest. Perhaps some of my poems might help them. They could choose for themselves which ones they liked the best. Then I gave them a challenge, "If you want to speak good English, you must be willing to do what it takes. You must pay the price to get what you want." The following are some of the poems I have written over the years:

PAYING THE PRICE

You want the best in life you say,
But are you willing the price to pay?
It's freedom you seek so you can live,
But what is it that you're willing to give?
Do you compromise and just say, "Ok,"
Or demand much more for a better day?
If you settle for less, I'm willing to bet,
You'll all deserve just what you get!
It's a law of life: "One seldom from life gets more
Than what he's willing to work and pay for."
For one thing is certain and this I know,
You'll only reap just what you sow.

THE WHITE ROSE

The rose, with heaven's fragrance,
  that blossoms pure and white.
Reflects celestial grandeur
  of love, and truth, and light.
It symbolizes virtue,
  faith, hope and charity.
It represents Christ's perfect life,
  and God's love for you and me.
Its beauty is a tribute
  to God's creative hand.
It flatters all of nature,
  and beautifies the land.
It's heavenly spirit matter,

the stuff from which it came.
Progress is it's trademark,
    and patience is its name.
This sacred holy flower
    has meaning that it should.
It represents the meaning
    of all that's pure and good.

THE NEXT TIME

The next time I run, I'll win the race.
The next time I love, I'll not disgrace.
The next time I ache, I'll not cry out.
The next time I'm blue, I will not pout.
The next time I'm tested, I will not cheat.
The next time I repent, T'will be complete.
Oh yes, the next time I start anew,
I will be sure to follow through.
But, what of now, before it's too late.
Shall I do it now, or Procrastinate?

TAKE A BREAK

When the day seems short and hurried
    and you feel all undone,
Just stop and give yourself a rest
    and have a little fun.
If in your daily labors,
    your back begins to ache,
Just stand up and look around
    and give yourself a break.
Weak or strong it matters not,
    you need a frequent breather.
Because, if you work yourself to death,
    you'll end up being neither.

That doesn't mean a man
  should loaf or up and quit.
I'm merely trying to recommend,
  one should relax himself a bit.
So when the day gets sort of hectic
  and you feel all undone,
Just stop and give yourself a rest
  and have a little fun.
Tell yourself a joke or two
  and laugh a little while.
Then return to meet the challenge
  and go the extra mile.

TWO SIDES TO LIFE

There are two sides to life. Which shall we choose?
The one that will heal, or the one that will bruise?
We're always confronted with evil and good;
Forever deciding if we shouldn't or should.
If it's right to be loyal or leave and forsake,
If it's better to give and not always take.
Do we have faith in God, or is it gold that we seek?
Are we puffed up in pride, or humble and meek?
Do we resolve to do right and make up our mind
To repent of our sins and leave them behind?
Are we a good neighbor going one mile more,
Or is helping them out too big of a chore.
Well, there's victory in life and there's also defeat.
We chose if we're honest or if we will cheat.
God in his wisdom will bless and rejoice
When each of his children make the right choice.
So remember both sides, for between them you will choose;
The one where you'll win or the one where you'll lose.

CHRISTMAS EVERY DAY

If Christmas ended sharply
  when clocks chimed midnight twelve's;
Me thinks I'd rather go and be
  one of Santa's little elves.
Cheering the kiddies one and all,
  aiding the old and gray;
To work and help to bring about
  a Christmas every day.
The age of twelve or ninety-two,
  it matters not at all.
If in your heart you're Santa's elf,
  you can have a year-long ball.
Oh, what a long year it would be
  if all we did was wait;
For one short day of love and cheer,
  one eve to stay up late.
Only one happy season where,
  the spirit of giving was high;
And bustling crowds in the square,
  find the perfect gift to buy.
Christmas comes but once a year,
  this small fact I know.
But in our hearts it can remain,
  through sunshine, rain and snow.

THANKS BEGINS WITH GIVING

Thanks begins with giving,
  each and every day;
The best of ourselves to others,
  in work or fun and play.
'Tis true, that word and deed
  treasure joys beyond compare,

But to be part of real Thanksgiving,
  the feeling must be there.
For the words that are long remembered,
  those so true and kind;
Are the thoughts that grew to action,
  and died not in the mind.
And a deed, in helping others,
  though quiet and small they seem
Is the thanks we can be giving
  if we'll act and not just dream.
Many a blessing is ours to count;
  bounties great and small.
Thanks to our Father who gave us life,
  and a Brother who saved us all;
For the freedom and the heritage we have
  and loved ones near and far;
For food we eat and clothes we wear,
  for the house and for the car.
God gives so much to you and me;
  large is our debt to pay.
Just thanking won't pay the bill;
  we must act on what we say.
With sincere thought and action,
  happy we may live.
Of ourselves, we give to others,
  but to God 'tis thanks we give.

VALENTINE

No arrow can carry the wishes I share;
Nor pigeon relay the message I bear.
A car is not able, a plane is too slow,
And a train cannot hold all my precious cargo.
Telegrams can't kiss through miles of line,
And a letter can't say, "Be My Valentine."

But, I can do all things that others can't do.
I can take true love and give it to you.

TIDES IN THE AFFAIRS OF MEN

The waves roll in with thundering tide,
  And then retreat as winds subside.
Such are the affairs and lives of men.
  Good fortune comes in and goes out again.
We're often stranded on lonely sands,
  But we're never lost from God's own hands.
The spirit is gone, the way seems dark;
  We know not the course on which to embark.
This is the plan of our mortal life,
  We're exploring worlds of struggle and strife.
It's His own way of building souls
  Of men searching for eternal goals.

WORDS OF WISDOM

A word to the young, a word to the wise,
  Don't fall prey to cunning lies.
You can't be strong and walk real tall,
  By trying to smoke or drink alcohol.
You can't get rich and pay your bills,
  By smoking joints or popping pills.
True joy and peace will pass you by,
  If you're shooting up and getting high.
Your troubles won't pass, your friends won't stay,
  And your body and mind will waste away.
So, if you want strength and want to be wise,
  Don't fall prey to cunning lies.
These Words of Wisdom are brief but true,
  Their test of worth is now up to you.

WORTH OF A SOUL

How many men have walked a mile,
One hundred or a thousand if need be,
To find their fortune, their glory or pride;
To conquer the mountain or sea?
How many have given life or limb,
Or a better part of their soul,
For a diamond, a treasure or even a purse,
Or a trophy for winning a goal?
If so many have run this kind of race
And paid the prices required,
Why haven't more helped others in need
Instead of quitting when tired.
The worth of a soul is greater than all
The riches we all can combine.
This is the measure our Savior taught
As he left the ninety and nine.

THAT SPECIAL ONE

The flowers are many and sweet fruits divine,
But I'll not taste of any, 'Till that special one's mine.
The shiniest of apples or the tastiest peach,
Is high in the tree top far out of reach.
It's not shaken loose to fall from the tree,
Because it's that special one just waiting for me;
To climb with precision and not just by chance ,
To carefully pick it from that high lofty branch.
Its freshness I'll cherish and protect with my life.
For such fruit is my goal in choosing a wife.
Such is the measure of each maiden's worth,
Like the freshness of flowers that cover the earth.
Their fragrance is virtue to be guarded with care,
Against those who'd pluck them in their sly, crafty snare.

Their beauty is priceless and if freely spent,
T'will leave their sweet petals all soiled and bent.
Such is the plight of those lining the road,
Drooped under the weight of their dark, dusty load.
But, as I travel the world, it's you that I'll find,
Not tarnished by others and then left behind,
But, far from the path when my searching is done,
I will sit down beside you my dear special one;
And nurture the love that God meant to be ,
For you see, special one, you're that special to me.

JUST ONE SWING

What I wouldn't do to have you here,
  My special love, my special Dear;
To gather you up, letting arms surround;
  To hold you close swinging you around.
Then sweep you off your feet I would,
  And hold you as close as I possibly could.
With your arms around my neck so tight,
  You'd laugh and scream with pure delight.
I'd spin and spin and 'round we'd go.
  I'd laugh and shout, "I love you so!"
There safely cradled in loving arms,
  You're free from fears and all that harms.
For moments, the world keeps rushing by,
  While we share a kiss and sigh and sigh.
After all this fun and spinning around
  I'd set you softly on the ground.
Then softly, gently, we'd hug and kiss;
  Sharing our love, our joy and bliss.
For this great treat so very nice,
  I'd work and toil and sacrifice.
I'd fight all beasts with my bare hands;
  I'd cross the desert's blistering sands.

I'd bare the winters snow and ice,
   For just one swing, T'would be so nice.
I'd search the jungles, walk on burning coals,
   Climb high mountains, swim rocky shoals.
No, there's nothing that I wouldn't do
   To share the thrill of swinging you.
You see, my dear, that's what you bring,
   To my heart that's yours, with just one swing.

FIRST HARSH WORDS

"The first harsh words never need be spoken,"
Was the counsel to bride and groom.
They are Satan's tools that hurt and divide,
And bring to all sorrow and gloom.
So resolve this day to bridle your tongue,
And never drive loved ones apart.
Only speak softness in loving tones,
The feelings and thoughts of your heart.

EATING HABITS

People's eating habits
   are the ways they eat their food.
Some people laugh and giggle,
   others sit and brood.
Some folks pick and nibble,
   others stir and mash.
Some just sip and sigh;
   while others slurp and splash.
Lots of people in a rush,
   eat in quite a furry.
They always spill and waste more time,
   as they try to hurry.
To some, eating is a sport

of intense competition.
They practice in-between their meals,
   by constant repetition.
A very few are quite polite,
   trying for improvements.
To them, it's all a symphony,
   with notes, and chords and movements.
"What we eat is what we are." '
   Tis a must we do it.
But as important to us all,
   is how we eat and chew it!

Summary

"Parting is such sweet sorrow."
- William Shakespeare

A Good-bye Party

It's difficult to write about something so special as my memories and experiences in China. I have grown to love my dear friends and MBA students and my special Tibetan students in the six week spoken English class. It seemed almost like a miracle that less than two months ago we needed an interpreter for the simplest things and now we could speak for hours about almost any topic with little difficulty. Their progress had been remarkable.

The Tibetan students all insisted on giving me a big dinner and party. Mr. Kunsung Gya of the Trace Foundation was coming to town and so the date was set. The party began in the morning in a beautiful restaurant next to the Bonsai tree museum on a small island in the middle of the river that completely circled Hefei City. It was the most beautiful time of year with all the flowers in bloom and the small jumping fish in the river. In the morning, we met in a large upper room that seated almost 40 people in a big circle. We had drinks, fruit, nuts etc., etc. About 1:30 p.m., after a large banquet downstairs, we went back upstairs where many sang beautiful songs. I was also asked to sing so I sang "The Battle of New Orleans" by Johnny Horton. Before I sang however, I explained the historical background and told them that the songwriter had been a high school history teacher and had written the song for his students. I admire that kind of teacher!

We left the island to go back to a restaurant on the USTC campus next to our apartment. There we had another huge banquet and ate from 6:00 p.m. to after 7:30 around three large tables with 12-14 people seated around each table. Everyone was engaged in lively conversation as they all went from table to table to toast each other. What a beautiful experience. Then without any warning, but I learned later this was the Tibetan custom, one of the men began to sing a lively song. When finished and the applause ended, table number two came back with an even more lively song. By the time I realized what was happening, our table was trying to outdo the first two.

For the next hour or so, one table after another sang in its turn a song that was different from others. I was amazed that they knew so many songs and that they could sing so well and with such gusto and spirit. The room literally vibrated with volume, melody and enthusiasm. Again, without knowing exactly who shifted the direction of the singing, several men encouraged Mary-Jo to get up in front of the group and sing a song. She did a beautiful job and sang as though she had sung professionally for years. Then she took her glass still half-filled with beverage and gave it to one of the male students at another table. It was obvious that he was now to take his turn, which he did.

Again, the performance was electrifying. This practice continued until all 36 people had sung a song. Some of them sang several times if the cup came back to them, which it sometimes did. Many of the men would put their hand over their one ear and sing the most beautiful melodies that they seemed to be making up on the spot. Some danced and almost told stories with their movements. As I listened to the first songs, I was stunned at the talent and quality of their voices. No music, just their singing, acting and dancing. Any one of them could have performed professionally and would have been received as a star! Over and over again, I thought to myself, I wish I had this party video taped. As a matter of fact, I wish I could have four or five cameras moving around the room to capture these special moments. It was that unique and that special.

Toward the end of the party or about 9:45 p.m., the glass came to Mary-Jo and I and we coaxed Jane to join us to sing "You Are My Sunshine." We did a pretty good job, but the cup never came back to us, but Jane was chosen to sing several times. Her voice, like the others, was clear and beautiful and she knew and sang songs in both English and Chinese. As a finale, everyone except the three us got up and sang and danced in Tibetan style. Mary-Jo and I enjoyed them through our tears of joy and appreciation. When they sang their last song to us, we all bid each other farewell. The night was over, but the spirit and feeling of the occasion lingered on for days.

Our daughter and son, Teresa and Jon, had been traveling with the American ILP Teachers from the International Language Program (ILP) to Xian and Beijing and had missed this event. It was the highlight of our whole experience in China. How we wished we could have shared it with them. We were so happy when just a few days later we were invited to another party the night of our last class. All of the ILP students were also invited and we had a marvelous time. Another big banquet with lots of singing and dancing the whole night long. At the end, the students presented me with a beautiful Budda tapestry, which now hangs in our home in the United States. As I carried it home on the plane with me, I thought over and over that I had come to China to experience the riches of China and I discovered Tibet and the Tibetan people as one of China's most beautiful treasures.

Your Dreams Can Come True

The day had finally arrived. This was to be the last class. Perhaps it was the last time that my Tibetan students and I would ever see each other in this life. Everyone had high hopes that this would not be the case, and we tried to assure each other that they would visit each other's hometown in the future. One day we would all have a reunion in the Tibetan capital of Lasa. This was everyone's dream.

I knew it would be difficult for me to get a visa to go to Lasa because of being an American. And it would be almost impossible for the Tibetan students to get a visa to enter the US. It was hard for them to leave and almost impossible to enter after the 9-11 terrorist attacks. Nevertheless, there was hope. People who love each other always have hope. During these two short months there had developed a bond of love and brotherhood among all of us in the class that was beautiful and real. But, it is very difficult to describe. Sometimes words cannot describe the most beautiful and the most special things; not Chinese, English or Tibetan words.

The class was over and everyone sat in silent realization that this was it. They were now on their own to go home to their families and students and to teach others how to speak English. It was hard for everyone to keep back the tears and not show their emotions, but we all were doing the best we could.

I braced myself to give my final words of advice and encouragement. Several times, I choked with emotion as I told the class how much I loved and appreciated them and complimented them on their efforts and dedication to follow my demands as a teacher. I continued, "Your dream to speak English fluently can and will come true. Just remember that wherever you are in your progress, your English is very good. Remind yourself that you are making excellent progress."

I spoke about their responsibility to share what they had learned with others. Not just the ability to speak English, but the ability to teach others how to speak English. Again, I challenged them to ask and tell their students, "Is there room for improvement? Of course there is room for improvement. You can even improve on your spoken Chinese. Did you ever stop to realize that even your spoken Chinese is not perfect? That's OK. My spoken English is not perfect and I'm a native English speaker. I too am always trying to improve my spoken English. Perhaps you may someday speak better English than I do, but maybe you don't believe it now. And, because you don't believe it, you don't have the confidence and you don't speak. Believe me, your English is good and it's getting better. As you progress, your self-esteem will improve and confidence will grow. Soon, your ability to speak and express yourself will surprise you.

"As I have told you before, there will be times when you will dream in English. Yes, dream in English. It's better than dreaming in color. When you dream in English you will know that you are making great progress in your spoken English. You will know that your dream to speak good English is actually coming true.

"Good luck to you! May all your dreams come true and may you live happily today and for ever after. I love you and I have confidence in you. Good bye for now."

Review: Recording & Scoring Your Results

These simple methods will remind you to do the activity, require you to keep a record of your progress and will show you where you are putting the most effort and where you need to improve. At the end of each day or week simply give an honest and objective evaluation of how you did during that day or week. Give yourself a number score from 0 to 10 in each activity area.

Remember that the numbers represent the following rating: 0 = no effort or failure to perform; 1 = very poor effort; 2 = little effort; 3 = not so good effort; 4 = below average; 5 = average; 6 = above average effort; 7 = very good effort; 8 = a lot of effort; 9 = excellent effort; 10 = perfect or maximum score available.

Add the total score for each day and then the total score for the whole week. You can follow your progress on the chart by plotting your cumulative average of your weekly scores. Just add up all the weekly scores and divide by the total number of weeks. That will give you your cumulative score. You may also like to prepare your own spreadsheet in your computer to quickly and easily calculate and plot these scores. If you are not sure how to do it, you can ask a friend who is a computer expert. **Daily Total Score** = the total of all the scores for each item. **Weekly Total Score** = the total of the scores for each day. **Average** = the overall total cumulative score divided by the number of days recorded.

Conclusion

So there you are. You have ten easy exercises and a method of recording and scoring your progress. You can do this on your own or with friends. It doesn't cost you anything, only some time and consistent effort and dedication. If you measure your progress each day, each week and each month you will visually see your progress. Let me remind you again, you are only competing with yourself, so be honest in your evaluation and scoring. These secrets are now your secrets and your success will depend on what you do with them.

About the Author

The author has written this book in an effort to help Chinese people think correctly and speak English fluently. He has applied basic business principles and practices to help people speak English. Readers can focus on those activities that will most help them speak fluently.

Dale Christensen was born in Shelley, Idaho, USA to Irven and Esther Christensen. He grew up in the small agricultural town of Blackfoot, Idaho (population 5,000) known as the "Potato Capital of the World." He graduated from Central High School in London, England and later earned his BS, BA and MBA degrees from Boston College in 1975 and has had valuable experience in several industries during his professional career.. He enjoyed a varied business career and taught MBA courses at the University of Science & Technology of China.

He has applied basic business principles and practices to help people speak English. The reader is able to focus on those activities that will most help them to speak fluently. He has authored several books including *The Shopping Center Acquisition Handbook* (1984), *Turning The Hearts* (Vol. 1-4, 1983-8), *Thoughts In Verse* (1982 & 2001), *Entrepreneur's Guide: The Ultimate Business & Learning Experience* (2001) and has written numerous articles for both *The Deseret News* and *The Daily Herald*.

Printed in Great Britain
by Amazon